SEMIOTEXT(E) INTERVENTION SERIES

© 2009 by The Invisible Committee
Originally published as *L'insurrection qui vient* by Editions La
Fabrique, Paris, 2007.

Published by Semiotext(e)
2007 Wilshire Blvd., Suite 427, Los Angeles, CA 90057
www.semiotexte.com

ISBN: 978-1-58435-080-4
Distributed by The MIT Press, Cambridge, Mass.
and London, England
Printed in the United States of America
10 9 8 7

The Invisible Committee

The Coming Insurrection

semiotext(e)
intervention
series □ 1

The book you hold in your hands has become the principle piece of evidence in an anti-terrorism case in France directed against nine individuals who were arrested on November 11, 2008, mostly in the village of Tarnac. They have been accused of "criminal association for the purposes of terrorist activity" on the grounds that they were to have participated in the sabotage of overhead electrical lines on France's national railways. Although only scant circumstantial evidence has been presented against the nine, the French Interior Minister has publically associated them with the emergent threat of an "ultra-left" movement, taking care to single out this book, described as a "manual for terrorism," which they are accused of authoring. What follows is the text of the book preceded by the first statement of the Invisible Committee since the arrests.

Contents

Introduction

A POINT OF CLARIFICATION

Everyone agrees. It's about to explode. It is acknowl-
edged, with a serious and self-important look, in the
corridors of the Assembly, just as yesterday it was
repeated in the cafés. There is a certain pleasure in
calculating the risks. Already, we are presented with a
detailed menu of preventive measures for securing
the territory. The New Years festivities take a decisive
turn—"Next year there'll be no oysters, enjoy them
while you can!" To prevent the celebrations from
being totally eclipsed by the traditional disorder,
36,000 cops and 16 helicopters are rushed out by
Alliot-Marie[1]—the same clown who, during the high
school demonstrations in December, tremulously
watched for the slightest sign of a Greek contamination, readying the police apparatus just in case. We
can discern more clearly every day, beneath the reas-
suring drone, the noise of preparations for open war.
It's impossible to ignore its cold and pragmatic
implementation, no longer even bothering to present
itself as an operation of pacification.

The newspapers conscientiously draw up the list of
causes for the sudden disquiet. There is the financial

---

1. Michèle Alliot-Marie, the French Interior Minister.

crisis, of course, with its booming unemployment, its share of hopelessness and of social plans, its Kerviel and Madoff scandals. There is the failure of the educational system, its dwindling production of workers and citizens, even with the children of the middle class as its raw material. There is the existence of a youth to which no political representation corresponds, a youth good for nothing but destroying the free bicycles that society so conscientiously put at their disposal.

None of these worrisome subjects should appear insurmountable in an era whose predominant mode of government is precisely the management of crises. Unless we consider that what power is confronting is neither just another crisis, nor just a succession of chronic problems, of more or less anticipated disturbances, but a singular peril: that a form of conflict has emerged, and positions have been taken up, that are no longer *manageable*.

Those who everywhere make up this peril have to ask themselves more than the trifling questions about causes, or the probabilities of inevitable movements and confrontations. They need to ask how, for instance, does the Greek chaos resonate in the French situation? An uprising here cannot be the simple transposition of what happened over there. Global civil war still has its local specificities. In France a situation of generalized rioting would provoke an explosion of another tenor.

The Greek rioters are faced with a weak state, while being able to take advantage of a strong popularity. One must not forget that it was against the Regime of the Colonels that, only thirty years ago, democracy reconstituted itself on the basis of a practice of political violence. This violence, whose memory is not so distant, still seems intuitive to most Greeks. Even the leaders of the socialist party have thrown a molotov or two in their youth. Yet classical politics is equipped with variants that know very well how to accommodate these practices and to extend their ideological rubbish to the very heart of the riot. If the Greek battle wasn't decided, and put down, in the streets— the police being visibly outflanked there—it's because its neutralization was played out elsewhere. There is nothing more draining, nothing more fatal, than this classical politics, with its dried up rituals, its thinking without thought, its little closed world.

In France, our most exalted socialist bureaucrats have never been anything other than shriveled husks filling up the halls of the Assembly. Here everything conspires to annihilate even the slightest form of political intensity. Which means that it is always possible to oppose the citizen to the delinquent in a quasi-linguistic operation that goes hand in hand with quasi-military operations. The riots of November 2005 and, in a different context, the social movements in the autumn of 2007, have already provided several precedents. The image of right wing students in Nanterre applauding as the police expelled their classmates offers a small glimpse of what the future holds in store.

It goes without saying that the attachment of the French to the state—the guarantor of universal values, the last rampart against the disaster—is a pathology that is difficult to undo. It's above all a fiction that no longer knows how to carry on. Our governors themselves increasingly consider it as a useless encumbrance because they, at least, take the conflict for what it is—*militarily*. They have no complex about sending in elite antiterrorist units to subdue riots, or to liberate a recycling center occupied by its workers. As the welfare state collapses, we see the emergence of a brute conflict between those who desire order and those who don't. Everything that French politics has been able to deactivate is in the process of unleashing itself. It will never be able to process all that it has repressed. In the advanced degree of social decomposition, we can count on the coming movement to find the necessary breath of nihilism. Which will not mean that it won't be exposed to other limits.

Revolutionary movements do not spread by contamination but by *resonance*. Something that is constituted here resonates with the shock wave emitted by something constituted over there. A body that resonates does so according to its own mode. An insurrection is not like a plague or a forest fire—a linear process which spreads from place to place after an initial spark. It rather takes the shape of a music, whose focal points, though dispersed in time and space, succeed in imposing the rhythm of their own vibrations, always taking on more density. To the point that any return to normal is no longer desirable or even imaginable.

When we speak of Empire we name the mechanisms of power that preventively and surgically stifle any revolutionary potential in a situation. In this sense, Empire is not an enemy that confronts us head-on. It is a rhythm that imposes itself, a way of dispensing and dispersing reality. Less an order of the world than its sad, heavy and militaristic liquidation.

What we mean by the party of insurgents is the sketching out of a completely other *composition*, an other side of reality, which from Greece to the French *banlieues*[2] is seeking its consistency.

It is now publicly understood that crisis situations are so many opportunities for the restructuring of domination. This is why Sarkozy can announce, without seeming to lie too much, that the financial crisis is "the end of a world," and that 2009 will see France enter a new era. This charade of an economic crisis is supposed to be a novelty: we are supposed to be in the dawn of a new epoch where we will all join together in fighting inequality and global warming. But for our generation—which was born in the crisis and has known nothing but economic, financial,

---

2. *Banlieue*—French ghettoes, usually located in the suburban periphery.

social and ecological crisis—this is rather difficult to accept. They won't fool us again, with another round of "Now we start all over again" and "It's just a question of tightening our belts for a little while." To tell the truth, the disastrous unemployment figures no longer arouse any feeling in us. Crisis is a means of governing. In a world that seems to hold together only through the infinite management of its own collapse.

What this war is being fought over is not various ways of managing society, but irreducible and irreconcilable ideas of happiness and their worlds. We know it, and so do the powers that be. The militant remnants that observe us—always more numerous, always more identifiable—are tearing out their hair trying to fit us into little compartments in their little heads. They hold out their arms to us the better to suffocate us, with their failures, their paralysis, their stupid problematics. From elections to "transitions," militants will never be anything other than that which distances us, each time a little farther, from the possibility of communism. Luckily we will accommodate neither treason nor deception for much longer.

The past has given us far too many bad answers for us not to see that the mistakes were in the questions themselves. There is no need to choose between the fetishism of spontaneity and organizational control; between the "come one, come all" of activist networks and the discipline of hierarchy; between acting desperately now and waiting desperately for later; between bracketing that which is to be lived and experimented in the name of a paradise that seems more and more like a hell the longer it is put off, and repeating, with a corpse-filled mouth, that planting carrots is enough to dispel this nightmare.

Organizations are obstacles to organizing ourselves.

In truth, there is no gap between what we are, what we do, and what we are becoming. Organizations— political or labor, fascist or anarchist—always begin by separating, practically, these aspects of existence. It's then easy for them to present their idiotic formalism as the sole remedy to this separation. To organize is not to give a structure to weakness. It is above all to form bonds—bonds that are by no means neutral—terrible bonds. The degree of organization is measured by the intensity of sharing—material *and* spiritual.

From now on, to materially organize for survival is to materially organize for attack. Everywhere, a new idea of communism is to be elaborated. In the shadows of bar rooms, in print shops, squats, farms, occupied gymnasiums, new complicities are to be born. These precious connivances must not be refused the necessary means for the deployment of their forces.

Here lies the truly revolutionary potentiality of the present. The increasingly frequent skirmishes have this formidable quality: that they are always an occasion for complicities of this type, sometimes ephemeral, but sometimes also unbetrayable. When a few thousand young people find the determination to assail this world, you'd have to be as stupid as a cop to seek out a financial trail, a leader, or a snitch.

Two centuries of capitalism and market nihilism have brought us to the most extreme alienations—from our selves, from others, from worlds. The fiction of the individual has decomposed at the same speed that it was becoming real. Children of the metropolis, we offer this wager: that it's in the most profound deprivation of existence, perpetually stifled, perpetually conjured away, that the possibility of communism resides.

When all is said and done, it's with an entire anthropology that we are at war. With the very idea of man.

Communism then, as presupposition *and* as experiment. Sharing of a sensibility *and* elaboration of sharing. The uncovering of what is common *and* the building of a force. Communism as the matrix of a meticulous, audacious assault on domination. As a call and as a name for all worlds resisting imperial pacification, all solidarities irreducible to the reign of commodities, all friendships assuming the necessities of war. COMMUNISM. We know it's a term to be used with caution. Not because, in the great parade of words, it may no longer be very fashionable. But because our worst enemies have used it, and continue to do so. We insist. Certain words are like battle-grounds: their meaning, revolutionary or reactionary, is a victory, to be torn from the jaws of struggle.

Deserting classical politics means facing up to war, which is also situated on the terrain of language. Or rather, in the way that words, gestures and life are inseparably linked. If one puts so much effort into imprisoning as terrorists a few young communists who are supposed to have participated in publishing *The Coming Insurrection*, it is not because of a "thought crime," but rather because they might embody a certain consistency between acts and thought. Something which is rarely treated with leniency.

What these people are accused of is not to have written a book, nor even to have physically attacked the sacrosanct flows that irrigate the metropolis. It's that they might possibly have confronted these flows with the density of a political thought and position. That an act could have made sense according to another consistency of the world than the deserted one of Empire. Anti-terrorism claims to attack the possible future of a "criminal association." But what is really being attacked is the future of the situation. The possibility that behind every grocer a few bad intentions are hiding, and behind every thought, the acts that it calls for. The possibility expressed by an idea of politics—anonymous but welcoming, contagious and uncontrollable—which cannot be relegated to the storeroom of freedom of expression.

There remains scarcely any doubt that youth will be the first to savagely confront power. These last few years, from the riots of Spring 2001 in Algeria to those of December 2008 in Greece, are nothing but a series of warning signs in this regard. Those who 30 or 40 years ago revolted against their parents will not hesitate to reduce this to a conflict between generations, if not to a predictable symptom of adolescence.

The only future of a "generation" is to be the preceding one. On a route that leads inevitably to the cemetery.

Tradition would have it that everything begins with a "social movement." Especially at a moment when the left, which has still not finished decomposing, hypocritically tries to regain its credibility in the streets. Except that in the streets it no longer has a monopoly. Just look at how, with each new mobilization of high school students—as with everything the left still dares to support—a rift continually widens between their whining demands and the level of violence and determination of the movement.

From this rift we must make a trench.

If we see a succession of movements hurrying one after the other, without leaving anything visible behind them, it must nonetheless be admitted that something persists. A powder trail links what in each event has not let itself be captured by the absurd temporality of the withdrawal of a new law, or some other pretext. In fits and starts, and in its own rhythm, we are seeing something like a force take shape. A force that does not serve its time but imposes it, silently.

It is no longer a matter of foretelling the collapse

or depicting the possibilities of joy. Whether it comes sooner or later, the point is to prepare for it. It's not a question of providing a schema for what an insurrection should be, but of taking the possibility of an uprising for what it never should have ceased being: a vital impulse of youth as much as a popular wisdom. If one knows how to move, the absence of a schema is not an obstacle but an opportunity. For the insurgents, it is the sole space that can guarantee the essential: keeping the initiative. What remains to be created, to be tended as one tends a fire, is a certain outlook, a certain tactical fever, which once it has emerged, even now, reveals itself as determinant—and a constant source of determination. Already certain questions have been revived that only yesterday may have seemed grotesque or outmoded; they need to be seized upon, not in order to respond to them definitively, but to make them live. Having posed them anew is not the least of the Greek uprising's virtues:

How does a situation of generalized rioting become an insurrectionary situation? What to do once the streets have been taken, once the police have been soundly defeated there? Do the parliaments still deserve to be attacked? What is the practical meaning of deposing power locally? How do we decide? How do we *subsist*?

How do we find each other?

— Invisible Committee, January 2009

The Coming Insurrection

From whatever angle you approach it, the present offers no way out. This is not the least of its virtues. From those who seek hope above all, it tears away every firm ground. Those who claim to have solutions are contradicted almost immediately. Everyone agrees that things can only get worse. "The future has no future" is the wisdom of an age that, for all its appearance of perfect normalcy, has reached the level of consciousness of the first punks.

The sphere of political representation has come to a close. From left to right, it's the same nothingness striking the pose of an emperor or a savior, the same sales assistants adjusting their discourse according to the findings of the latest surveys. Those who still vote seem to have no other intention than to desecrate the ballot box by voting as a pure act of protest. We're beginning to suspect that it's only *against voting itself* that people continue to vote. Nothing we're being shown is adequate to the situation, not by far. In its very silence, the populace seems infinitely more mature than all these puppets bickering among themselves about how to govern it. The ramblings of any Belleville *chibani*[1] contain more wisdom than all the declarations of our so-called leaders. The lid on the social kettle is shut triple-tight, and the pressure inside continues to build. From out of Argentina, the specter of *Que Se Vayan Todos*[2] is beginning to seriously haunt the ruling class.

The flames of November 2005 still flicker in everyone's minds. Those first joyous fires were the baptism of a decade full of promise. The media fable of "*banlieue* vs. the Republic" may work, but what it gains in effectiveness it loses in truth. Fires were lit in the city centers, but this news was methodically suppressed. Whole streets in Barcelona burned in solidarity, but no one knew about it apart from the people living there. And it's not even true that the country has stopped burning. Many different profiles can be found among the arrested, with little that unites them besides a hatred for existing society—not class, race, or even neighborhood. What was new wasn't the "*banlieue* revolt," since that was already going on in the '80s, but the break with its established forms. These assailants no longer listen to anybody, neither to their Big

---

1. *Chibani* is Arabic for old man, here referring to the old men who play backgammon in the cafes of Belleville, a largely immigrant neighborhood in Paris.

2. *They All Must Go!*—the chant of the 2001 Argentine rebellion.

Brothers and Big Sisters, nor to the community organizations charged with overseeing the return to normal. No "SOS Racism"[3] could sink its cancerous roots into this event, whose apparent conclusion can be credited only to fatigue, falsification and the media *omertà*.[4] This whole series of nocturnal vandalisms and anonymous attacks, this wordless destruction, has widened the breach between politics and the political. No one can honestly deny the obvious: this was an assault that made no demands, a threat without a message, and it had nothing to do with "politics." One would have to be oblivious to the autonomous youth movements of the last 30 years not to see the purely political character of this resolute negation of politics. Like lost children we trashed the prized trinkets of a society that deserves no more respect than the monuments of Paris at the end of the Bloody Week[5]—and knows it.

There will be no *social* solution to the present situation. First, because the vague aggregate of social milieus, institutions, and individualized bubbles that is called, with a touch of *antiphrasis*, "society," has no

---

3. A French Anti-Racist NGO set up by Francois Mitterand's Socialist Party in the '80s.

4. The mafia "code of silence": absolutely no cooperation with state authorities or reliance on their services.

5. The battle that crushed the Paris Commune of 1871, during which hundreds of buildings around Paris were torched by the communards.

consistency. Second, because there's no longer any language for common experience. And we cannot share wealth if we do not share a language. It took half a century of struggle around the Enlightenment to make the French Revolution possible, and a century of struggle around work to give birth to the fearsome "welfare state." Struggles create the language in which a new order expresses itself. But there is nothing like that today. Europe is now a continent gone broke that shops secretly at discount stores and has to fly budget airlines if it wants to travel at all. No "problems" framed in social terms admit of a solution. The questions of "pensions," of "job security," of "young people" and their "violence" can only be held in suspense while the situation these words serve to cover up is continually policed for signs of further unrest. Nothing can make it an attractive prospect to wipe the asses of pensioners for minimum wage. Those who have found less humiliation and more advantage in a life of crime than in sweeping floors will not turn in their weapons, and prison won't teach them to love society. Cuts to their monthly pensions will undermine the desperate pleasure-seeking of hordes of retirees, making them stew and splutter about the refusal to work among an ever larger segment of youth. And finally, no guaranteed income granted the day after a quasi-uprising will be able to lay the foundation of a new New Deal, a new pact, a new peace. The social feeling has already evaporated too much for that.

As an attempted solution, the pressure to ensure that *nothing happens*, together with police surveillance of the territory, will only intensify. The unmanned drone that flew over Seine-Saint-Denis[6] last July 14th—as the police later confirmed—presents a much more vivid image of the future than all the fuzzy humanistic projections. That they were careful to assure us that the drone was unarmed gives us a clear indication of the road we're headed down. The territory will be partitioned into ever more restricted zones. Highways built around the borders of "problem neighborhoods" already form invisible walls closing off those areas from the middle-class subdivisions. Whatever defenders of the Republic may think, the control of neighborhoods "by the community" is manifestly the most effective means available. The purely metropolitan sections of the country, the main city centers, will go about their opulent lives in an ever more crafty, ever more sophisticated, ever more shimmering deconstruction. They will illuminate the whole planet with their glaring neon lights, as the patrols of the BAC[7] and private security companies (i.e. paramilitary

---

6. *Banlieue* northeast of Paris, where, on October 27, 2005, two teenagers were killed as they fled the police, setting off the 2005 riots.

7. Brigade Anti-Criminalité plainclothes cops who act as an anti-gang force in the banlieues but also in demonstrations, often operating as a gang themselves in competition for territory and resources.

units) proliferate under the umbrella of an increasingly shameless judicial protection.

The impasse of the present, everywhere in evidence, is everywhere denied. There will be no end of psychologists, sociologists, and literary hacks applying themselves to the case, each with a specialized jargon from which the conclusions are especially absent. It's enough to listen to the songs of the times—the asinine "alt-folk" where the petty bourgeoisie dissects the state of its soul, next to declarations of war from Mafia K'1 Fry[8]—to know that a certain coexistence will end soon, that a decision is near.

This book is signed in the name of an imaginary collective. Its contributors are not its authors. They were content merely to introduce a little order into the common-places of our time, collecting some of the murmurings around barroom tables and behind closed bedroom doors. They've done nothing more than lay down a few necessary truths, whose universal repression fills psychiatric hospitals with patients, and eyes with pain. They've made themselves scribes of the situation. It's the privileged feature of radical circumstances that a rigorous application of logic leads to revolution. It's enough just to say what is before our eyes and not to shrink from the conclusions.

---

8. Popular French rap group.

First Circle

"I AM WHAT I AM"

"I AM WHAT I AM." This is marketing's latest offering to the world, the final stage in the development of advertising, far beyond all the exhortations to be different, to be oneself and drink Pepsi. Decades of concepts in order to get where we are, to arrive at pure tautology. I = I. He's running on a treadmill in front of the mirror in his gym. She's coming back from work behind the wheel of her Smart car. Will they meet?

"I AM WHAT I AM." My body belongs to me. I am me, you are you, and *something's wrong.* Mass personalization. Individualization of all conditions—life, work and misery. Diffuse schizophrenia. Rampant depression. Atomization into fine paranoiac particles. Hysterization of contact. The more I want to be me, the more I feel an emptiness. The more I express myself, the more I am drained. The more I run after myself, the more tired I get. We treat our Self like a boring box ofice. We've become our own representatives in a strange commerce, guarantors of a personalization that feels, in the end, a lot more like an amputation. We insure our selves to the point of bankruptcy, with a more or less disguised clumsiness.

Meanwhile, I *manage*. The quest for a self, my blog, my apartment, the latest fashionable crap, relationship dramas, who's fucking who... whatever prosthesis it takes to hold onto an "I"! If "society" hadn't become such a definitive abstraction, then it would denote all the existential crutches that allow me to keep dragging on, the ensemble of dependencies I've contracted as the price of my identity. *The handicapped are the model citizens of tomorrow.* It's not without foresight that the associations exploiting them today demand that they be granted a "subsistence income."

The injunction, everywhere, to "be someone" maintains the pathological state that makes this society necessary. The injunction to be strong produces the very weakness by which it maintains itself, so that *everything seems to take on a therapeutic character*, even working, even love. All those "How's it goings?" that we exchange give the impression of a society composed of patients taking each other's temperature. Sociability is now made up of a thousand little niches, a thousand little refuges where you can take shelter. Where it's always better than the bitter cold outside. Where everything's false, since it's all just a pretext for getting warmed up. Where nothing can happen since we're all too busy shivering silently together. Soon this society will only be held together by the mere tension of all the social atoms straining towards an illusory cure. It's a power plant that runs its turbines on a gigantic reservoir of unwept tears, always on the verge of spilling over.

"I AM WHAT I AM." Never has domination found such an innocent-sounding slogan. The maintenance of the self in a permanent state of deterioration, in a chronic state of near-collapse, is the best-kept secret of the present order of things. The weak, depressed, self-critical, virtual self is essentially that endlessly adaptable subject required by the ceaseless innovation of production, the accelerated obsolescence of technologies, the constant overturning of social norms, and generalized flexibility. It is at the same time the most voracious consumer and, paradoxically, the *most productive self*, the one that will most eagerly and energetically throw itself into the slightest *project*, only to return later to its original larval state.

"WHAT AM I," then? Since childhood, I've been involved with flows of milk, smells, stories, sounds, emotions, nursery rhymes, substances, gestures, ideas, impressions, gazes, songs, and foods. What am I? Tied in every way to places, sufferings, ancestors, friends, loves, events, languages, memories, to all kinds of things that obviously *are not me*. Everything that attaches me to the world, all the links that constitute me, all the forces that compose me don't form an identity, a thing displayable on cue, but a singular, shared, living *existence*, from which emerges—at certain times and places—that being which says "I." Our feeling of inconsistency is simply the consequence of this foolish belief in the permanence of the self and of the little care we give to what makes us what we are.

It's dizzying to see Reebok's "I AM WHAT I AM" enthroned atop a Shanghai skyscraper. The West everywhere rolls out its favorite Trojan horse: the exasperating antimony between the self and the world, the individual and the group, between attachment and freedom. Freedom isn't the act of shedding our attachments, but the *practical* capacity to work on them, to move around in their space, to form or dissolve them. The family only exists as a family, that is, as a hell, for those who've quit trying to alter its debilitating mechanisms, or don't know how to. The freedom *to uproot oneself* has always been a phantasmic freedom. We can't rid ourselves of what binds us without at the same time losing the very thing to which our forces would be applied.

"I AM WHAT I AM," then, is not simply a lie, a simple advertising campaign, but a *military* campaign, a war cry directed against everything that exists *between* beings, against everything that circulates indistinctly, everything that invisibly links them, everything that prevents complete desolation, against everything that makes us *exist*, and ensures that the whole world doesn't everywhere have the look and feel of a highway, an amusement park or a new town: pure boredom, passionless but well-ordered, empty, frozen space, where nothing moves apart from registered bodies, molecular automobiles, and ideal commodities.

France wouldn't be the land of anxiety pills that it's become, the paradise of anti-depressants, the Mecca of neurosis, if it weren't also the European champion of hourly productivity. Sickness, fatigue, depression, can be seen as the *individual* symptoms of what needs to be cured. They contribute to the maintenance of the existing order, to my docile adjustment to idiotic norms, and to the modernization of my crutches. They specify the selection of my opportune, compliant, and productive tendencies, as well as those that must be gently discarded. "It's never too late to change, you know." But taken as *facts*, my failings can also lead to the dismantling of the hypothesis of the self. They then become acts of resistance in the current war. They become a rebellion and a force against everything that conspires to normalize us, to amputate us. *The self is not some thing within us that is in a state of crisis; it is the form they mean to stamp upon us.* They want to make our self something sharply defined, separate, assessable in terms of qualities, controllable, when in fact we are creatures among creatures, singularities among similars, living flesh weaving the flesh of the world. Contrary to what has been repeated to us since childhood, intelligence doesn't mean knowing how to adapt—or if that is a kind of intelligence, it's the intelligence of slaves. *Our inadaptability*, our fatigue, are only *problems* from the standpoint of what aims to subjugate us. They indicate rather a starting point, a meeting point, for new complicities. They reveal a landscape more damaged, but infinitely more sharable than all the fantasy lands this society maintains for its purposes.

We are not depressed; we're on strike. For those who refuse to manage themselves, "depression" is not a state but a passage, a bowing out, a sidestep towards a *political* disaffiliation. From then on medication and the police are the only possible forms of conciliation. This is why the present society doesn't hesitate to impose Ritalin on its overactive children, or to strap people into lifelong dependence on pharmaceuticals, and why it claims to be able to detect "behavioral disorders" at age three. Because everywhere the hypothesis of the self is beginning to crack.

"ENTERTAINMENT IS A VITAL NEED"

A government that declares a state of emergency against fifteen-year-old kids. A country that takes refuge in the arms of a football team. A cop in a hospital bed, complaining about being the victim of "assault." A prefect issuing a decree against the building of tree houses. Two ten year olds, in Chelles, charged with burning down a video game arcade. Our era excels in a certain situational absurdity that it never seems to recognize. The truth is that the plaintive, indignant tones of the news media are unable to stifle the burst of laughter that greets these headlines.

A burst of laughter is the only appropriate response to all the serious "questions" posed by news analysts. To take the most banal: there is no "immigration question." Who still grows up where they were born? Who lives where they grew up? Who works where they live? Who lives where their ancestors did? And to whom do the children of this era belong, to television or their parents? The truth is that we have been completely torn from any belonging, we are no longer from anywhere, and the result, in addition to a new disposition to tourism, is an undeniable suffering. Our history is one of colonizations, of migrations, of wars, of exiles, of the destruction of all roots. It's the story of everything that has made us foreigners in this world, guests in our own family. We have been expropriated from our own language by education, from our songs by reality TV contests, from our flesh by mass pornography, from our city by the police, and from our friends by wage-labor. To this we should add, in France, the relentless, age-old work of individualization by the power of the state, that classifies, compares, disciplines and separates its subjects starting from a very young age, that instinctively grinds down any solidarities that escape it until nothing remains except citizenship—a pure, phantasmic sense of belonging to the Republic. The Frenchman, more than anyone else, is the embodiment of the dispossessed, the destitute. His hatred of foreigners is of a piece with his hatred of himself *as a foreigner*. The mixture of jealousy and fear he feels toward the "*cités*"[1] expresses nothing but his resentment for all he has lost. He can't help envying these so-called "problem" neighborhoods where there still persists a bit of communal life, a few links between beings, some solidarities not controlled by the state, an informal economy, an organization that is not yet

1. A housing project, typically in impoverished areas like the *banlieues*.

detached from those who organize themselves. We have arrived at a point of privation where the only way to feel French is to curse the immigrants and those who are *more visibly foreign*. In this country, the immigrants assume a curious position of sovereignty: *if they weren't here, the French might stop existing.*

France is a product of its schools, and not the inverse. We live in an excessively scholastic country, where one remembers taking the baccalauréat exam as a defining moment. Where retired people still tell you about their failure, forty years earlier, in such and such an exam, and how it screwed up their whole career, their whole life. For a century and a half, the national school system has been producing a type of state subjectivity that stands out among all others. People who accept competition provided the playing field is level. Who expect in life that each person be rewarded as in a contest, according to their merit. Who always ask permission before taking. Who silently respect culture, the rules, and those with the best grades. Even their attachment to their great critical intellectuals and their rejection of capitalism are stamped by this love of school. It's this construction of subjectivities by the state that is breaking down, every day a little more, with the decline of the scholarly institutions. The reappearance, over the past twenty years, of a school and a culture of the street, in competition with the school of the Republic and its cardboard culture, is the most deepest trauma that French universalism is presently undergoing. On this point, there is no disagreement between the extreme right and the most virulent left. The name Jules Ferry—Minister of Thiers during the crushing of the Commune and theoretician of colonization—should be enough however to render this institution suspect.[2]

When we see teachers from some "citizens' vigilance committee" come on the evening news to whine about *their* school being burned down, we remember how many times, as children, we dreamed of doing exactly this. When we hear a leftist intellectual venting about the barbarism of groups of kids harassing passersby in the street, shoplifting, burning cars, and playing cat and mouse with riot police, we remember what they said about the greasers in the '50s or, better, the apaches in the "Belle Époque:" "The generic name *apaches*," writes a judge at the Seine tribunal in 1907, "has for the past few years been a way of labeling all dangerous individuals, enemies of society, without nation or family, deserters of all duties, ready for the most audacious confrontations, and for any sort of attack on persons and properties." These gangs who flee work, who adopt

---

2. The Ferry laws—founding France's secular and republican system of education—were named after Jules Ferry who initially proposed them in 1881.

the names of their neighborhoods, and confront the police are the nightmare of the good, individualized French citizen: they embody everything he has renounced, all the possible joy he will never experience. There is something impertinent about *existing* in a country where a child singing as she pleases is inevitably silenced with a "Stop, you're going to stir things up," where scholastic castration unleashes floods of well-mannered employees. The aura that persists around Mesrine[3] has less to do with his uprightness and his audacity than with the fact that he took it upon himself to enact vengeance on what we should all avenge. Or rather, on what we should avenge *directly*, when instead we continue to hesitate and defer endlessly. Because there is no doubt that in a thousand imperceptible and undercover ways, in all sorts of slanderous remarks, in every spiteful little expression and venomous politeness, the Frenchman continues to avenge, permanently and against everyone, the fact that he's resigned himself to being crushed. It was about time that *Fuck the police*! replaced *Yes sir, officer*! In this sense, the open hostility of certain gangs only expresses, in a slightly less muffled way, the poisonous atmosphere, the rotten spirit, the desire for a salvational destruction by which the country is consumed.

---

3. A legendary French outlaw, 1936–1979.

To call this population of strangers in the midst of which we live "society" is such a usurpation that even sociologists wonder if they should abandon a concept that was, for a century, their bread and butter. Now they prefer the metaphor of a *network* to describe the connection of cybernetic solitudes, the intermeshing of weak interactions under names like "colleague," "contact," "buddy," "acquaintance," or "date." Such networks sometimes condense into a *milieu*, where nothing is shared but codes, and where nothing is played out except the incessant recomposition of identity.

It would be a waste of time to detail all that is moribund in existing social relations. They say the family is coming back, the couple is coming back. But the family that's coming back is not the same one that went away. Its return is nothing but a deepening of the prevailing separation that it serves to mask, becoming what it is through this masquerade. Everyone can testify to the doses of sadness condensed from year to year in family gatherings, the forced smiles, the awkwardness of seeing everyone pretending in vain, the feeling that a corpse is lying there on the table, and everyone acting as though it were nothing. From flirtation to divorce, from cohabitation to stepfamilies, everyone feels the inanity of the sad family nucleus, but most seem to believe that it would be sadder still to give it up. The family is no longer so much the suffocation of maternal control or the patriarchy of beatings as it is this infantile abandon to a fuzzy dependency, where everything is familiar, this carefree moment in the face of a world that nobody can deny is breaking down, a world where "becoming self-sufficient" is a euphemism for "finding a boss." They want to use the "familiarity" of the biological family as an excuse to undermine anything that burns passionately within us and, under the pretext that they raised us, make us renounce the possibility of growing up, as well as everything that is serious in childhood. We need to guard against such corrosion.

The couple is like the final stage of the great social debacle. It's the oasis in the middle of the human desert. Under the auspices of "intimacy," we come to it looking for everything that has so obviously deserted contemporary social relations: warmth, simplicity, truth, a life without theater or spectator. But once the romantic enchantment has passed, "intimacy" strips itself bare: it is itself a social invention, it speaks the language of glamour magazines and psychology; like everything else, it is bolstered with strategies to the point of nausea. There is no more truth here than elsewhere; here too lies and the laws of estrangement dominate. And when, by good fortune, one discovers this truth, it demands a sharing that belies the very form of the couple. What allows beings to love each other is also what makes them lovable, and ruins the utopia of autism-for-two.

In reality, the decomposition of all social forms is a blessing. It is for us the ideal condition for a wild, massive experimentation with new arrangements, new fidelities. The famous "parental resignation" has imposed on us a confrontation with the world that demands a precocious lucidity, and foreshadows lovely revolts to come. In the death of the couple, we see the birth of troubling forms of collective affectivity, now that sex is all used up and masculinity and femininity parade around in such moth-eaten clothes, now that three decades of non-stop pornographic innovation have exhausted all the allure of transgression and liberation. We count on making that which is unconditional in relationships the armor of a political solidarity as impenetrable to state interference as a gypsy camp. There is no reason that the interminable subsidies that numerous relatives are compelled to offload onto their proletarianized progeny can't become a form of patronage in favor of social subversion. "Becoming autonomous," could just as easily mean learning to fight in the street, to occupy empty houses, to cease working, to love each other madly, and to shoplift.

Third Circle

"LIFE, HEALTH AND LOVE ARE PRECARIOUS— WHY SHOULD WORK BE AN EXCEPTION?"

No question is more confused, in France, than the question of work. No relation is more disfigured than the one between the French and work. Go to Andalusia, to Algeria, to Naples. They despise work, profoundly. Go to Germany, to the United States, to Japan. They revere work. Things are changing, it's true. There are plenty of *otaku* in Japan, *frohe Arbeitslose* in Germany and *workaholics* in Andalusia. But for the time being these are only curiosities. In France, we get down on all fours to climb the ladders of hierarchy, but privately flatter ourselves that we don't really give a shit. We stay at work until ten o'clock in the evening when we're swamped, but we've never had any scruples about stealing office supplies here and there, or carting off the inventory in order to resell it later. We hate bosses, but we want to be employed at any cost. To have a job is an honor, yet working is a sign of servility. In short: the perfect clinical illustration of hysteria. We love while hating, we hate while loving. And we all know the stupor and confusion that strike the hysteric when he loses his victim—his master. More often than not, he doesn't get over it.

This neurosis is the basis on which successive governments could declare war on joblessness, claiming to wage an "employment battle" while ex-managers camped with their cell phones in Red Cross shelters along the banks of the Seine. While the Department of Labor was massively manipulating its statistics in order to bring unemployment numbers below two million. While welfare checks and drug dealing were the only guarantees, as the French state has recognized, against the possibility of a social explosion at any moment. It's the psychic economy of the French as much as the political stability of the country that is at stake in the maintenance of the workerist fiction.

Excuse us if we don't give a fuck.

We belong to a generation that lives *very well* in this fiction. That has never counted on either a pension or the right to work, let alone rights *at* work. That isn't even "precarious," as the most advanced factions of the militant left like to theorize, because to be precarious is still to define oneself in relation to the sphere of work, that is, *to its decomposition*. We accept the necessity of finding money, by whatever means, because it is currently impossible to do without it, but we reject the necessity of working. Besides, we don't work anymore: *we do our time*. Business is not a place where we exist, it's a place we pass through. We aren't cynical, we are just unwilling to be deceived. All these discourses on motivation, quality and personal investment pass us by, to the great dismay of personnel managers. They say we are disappointed by business, that it failed to honor our parents' loyalty, that it let them go too quickly. They are lying. To be disappointed, one must have hoped for something. And we have never hoped for anything from business: we see it for what it is and for what it has always been, a fool's game of varying degrees of comfort. With regard to our parents, our only regret is that they fell into the trap, at least the ones who believed.

The sentimental confusion that surrounds the question of work can be explained thus: the notion of work has always included two contradictory *dimensions*: a dimension of *exploitation* and a dimension of *participation*. Exploitation of individual and collective labor power through the private or social appropriation of surplus value; participation in a common effort through the relations linking those who cooperate in the universe of production. These two dimensions are perversely confused in the notion of work, which explains workers' indifference, at the end of the day, to both Marxist rhetoric—which denies the dimension of participation—and managerial rhetoric—which denies the dimension of exploitation. Hence the ambivalence of the relation of work, which is shameful insofar as it makes us strangers to what we are doing, and—at the same time—adored, insofar as a part of ourselves is brought into play. The disaster has already occurred: it resides in everything that had to be destroyed, in all those who had to be uprooted, in order for work to end up as *the only way of existing*. The horror of work is less in the work itself than in the methodical ravaging, for centuries, of all that isn't work: the familiarities of one's neighborhood and trade, of one's village, of struggle, of kinship, our attachment to places, to beings, to the seasons, to ways of doing and speaking.

Here lies the present paradox: work has totally triumphed over all other ways of existing, as the same time as workers have become superfluous. Gains in productivity, outsourcing, mechanization, automated and digital production have so progressed that they have almost reduced to zero the quantity of living labor necessary in the manufacture of any product. We are living the paradox of a society of workers without work, where entertainment, consumption and leisure only underscore the lack from which they are supposed to distract us. The mine at Carmaux, famous for a century of violent strikes, has now been converted into Cape Discovery. It's an entertainment "multiplex" for skateboarding and biking, distinguished by a "Mining Museum" in which methane blasts are simulated for vacationers.

In corporations, work is divided in an increasingly visible way into highly skilled positions of research, conception, control, coordination and communication which deploy all the knowledge necessary for the new, cybernetic production process, and unskilled positions for the maintenance and monitering of this process. The first are few in number, very well paid and thus so coveted that the minority who occupy these positions will do anything to avoid losing them. They and their work are effectively bound in one anxious embrace. Managers, scientists, lobbyists, researchers, programmers, developers, consultants and engineers, literally *never* stop working. Even their sex lives serve to augment productivity. A Human Resources philosopher writes, "[t]he most creative businesses are the ones with the greatest number of intimate relations." "Business associates," a Daimler-Benz Human Resources Manager confirms, "are an important part of the business's capital [...] Their motivation, their know-how, their capacity to innovate and their attention to clients' desires constitute the raw material of innovative services [...] Their behavior, their social and emotional competence, are a growing factor in the evaluation of their work [...] This will no longer be evaluated in terms of number of hours on the job, but on the basis of objectives attained and quality of results. They are entrepreneurs."

The series of tasks that can't be delegated to automation form a nebulous cluster of positions that, because they cannot be occupied by machines, are occupied by any old human—warehousemen, stock people, assembly line workers, seasonal workers, etc. This flexible, undifferentiated workforce that moves from one task to the next and never stays long in a business can no longer even consolidate itself as a force, being outside the center of the production process and employed to plug the holes of what has not yet been mechanized, as if pulverized in a multitude of interstices. The temp is the figure of the worker who is no longer a worker, who no longer has a *trade*—but only abilities that he sells where he can— and whose very availability is also a kind of work.

On the margins of this workforce that is effective and necessary for the functioning of the machine, is a growing majority that has become superfluous, that is certainly useful to the flow of production but not much else, which introduces the risk that, in its idleness, it will set about sabotaging the machine. The menace of a general demobilization is the specter that haunts the present system of production. Not everybody responds to the question "Why work?" in the same way as this ex-welfare recipient: "For my well-being. I have to keep myself busy." *There is a serious risk that we will end up finding a good use for our very idleness.* This floating population must somehow be kept occupied. But to this day they have not found a better disciplinary method than wages. It's therefore necessary to pursue the dismantling of "social gains" so that the most rest-less ones, those who will only surrender when faced with the alternative of dying of hunger or stagnating in jail, are lured back to the bosom of wage-labor. The burgeoning slave trade in "personal services" must continue: cleaning, catering, massage, domestic nursing, prostitution, tutoring, therapy, psycholog-ical aid, etc. This is accompanied by a continual raising of the standards of security, hygiene, control, and culture, and by an accelerated recycling of fashions, all of which establish the need for such services. In Rouen, we now have "human parking meters:" peo-ple who wait around on the street and deliver you your parking slip, and, if it's raining, will even rent you an umbrella.

The order of work was the order of a world. The evi-dence of its ruin is paralyzing to those who dread what will come after. Today work is tied less to the *economic* necessity of producing goods than to the *political* necessity of producing producers and con-sumers, and of preserving by any means necessary the order of work. Producing *oneself* is becoming the dominant occupation of a society where production no longer has an object: like a carpenter who's been evicted from his shop and in desperation sets about hammering and sawing himself. All these young people smiling for their job interviews, who have their teeth whitened to give them an edge, who go to nightclubs to boost their company spirit, who learn English to advance their careers, who get divorced or married to move up the ladder, who take courses in leadership or practice "self-improvement" in order to better "manage conflicts"—"the most intimate 'self-improvement'," says one guru, "will lead to increased emotional stability, to smoother and more open relationships, to sharper intellectual focus, and therefore to a better economic performance." This swarming little crowd that waits impatiently to be hired while doing whatever it can to seem natural is the result of an attempt to rescue the order of work through an ethos of *mobility*. To be mobilized is to relate to work not as an activity but as a *possibility*. If the unemployed person removes his piercings, goes to the barber and keeps himself busy with "projects," if he really works on his "employability," as they say, it's because this is how he demonstrates his mobility. Mobility is this slight detachment from the self, this minimal disconnection from what constitutes us, this condition of strangeness whereby the self can now be taken up as an object of work, and it now becomes possible to sell *oneself* rather than one's labor power, to be remunerated not for what one does but for what one is, for our exquisite mastery of social codes, for our relational talents, for our smile and our way of presenting ourselves. This is the new standard of socialization. Mobility brings about a fusion of the two contradictory poles of work: here we participate in our own exploitation, and all participation is exploited. Ideally, you are yourself a little business, your own boss, your own product. Whether one is working or not, it's a question of generating contacts, abilities, networking, in short: "human capital." The planetary injunction to mobilize at the slightest pretext—cancer, "terrorism," an earthquake, the homeless—sums up the reigning powers' determination to maintain the reign of work beyond its physical disappearance.

The present production apparatus is therefore, on the one hand, a gigantic machine for psychic and physical mobilization, for sucking the energy of humans that have become superfluous, and, on the other hand, a *sorting* machine that allocates survival to conpliant subjectivities and rejects all "problem individuals," all those who embody another use of life and, in this way, resist the machine. On the one hand, ghosts are brought to life, and on the other, the living are left to die. This is the properly political function of the contemporary production apparatus.

To organize beyond and against work, to collectively desert the regime of mobility, to demonstrate the existence of a vitality and a discipline precisely *in demobilization* is a crime for which a civilization on its knees is not about to forgive us. In fact, though, it's the only way to survive it.

Fourth Circle

"MORE SIMPLE, MORE FUN, MORE MOBILE, MORE SECURE!"

We've heard enough about the "city" and the "country," and particularly about the supposed ancient opposition between the two. From up close or from afar, what surrounds us looks nothing like that: it is one single urban cloth, without form or order, a bleak zone, endless and undefined, a global continuum of museum-like hypercenters and natural parks, of enormous suburban housing developments and massive agricultural projects, industrial zones and subdivisions, country inns and trendy bars: the metropolis. Certainly the ancient city existed, as did the cities of medieval and modern times. But there is no such thing as a metropolitan city. All territory is subsumed by the metropolis. Everything occupies the same space, if not geographically then through the intermeshing of its networks.

It's because the city has finally disappeared that it has now become fetishized, as history. The factory buildings of Lille become concert halls. The rebuilt concrete core of Le Havre is now a UNESCO World Heritage sire. In Beijing, the hutongs surrounding the Forbidden City were demolished, replaced by fake versions, placed a little farther out, on display for sightseers. In Troyes they paste half-timber facades onto cinderblock buildings, a type of pastiche that resembles the Victorian shops at Disneyland Paris more than anything else. The old historic centers, once hotbeds of revolutionary sedition, are now wisely integrated into the organizational diagram of the metropolis. They've been given over to tourism and conspicuous consumption. They are the fairy-tale commodity islands, propped up by their expos and decorations, and by force if necessary. The oppressive sentimentality of every "Christmas Village" is offset by ever more security guards and city patrols. Control has a wonderful way of integrating itself into the commodity landscape, showing its authoritarian face to anyone who wants to see it. It's an age of fusions, of muzak, telescoping police batons and cotton candy. Equal parts police surveillance and enchantment!

This taste for the "authentic," and for the control that goes with it, accompanies the petty bourgeoisie in its colonization of working class neighborhoods. Pushed out of the city centers, they find on the frontiers the kind of "neighborhood feeling" they missed in the prefab houses of suburbia. By chasing out the poor people, the cars, and the immigrants, by making it *tidy*, by getting rid of all the germs, the petty bourgeoisie wipes out the very thing it came looking for. A police officer and a garbage man shake hands in a picture on a town billboard, and the slogan reads: "Montauban—Clean City."

The same sense of decency that obliges urbanists to stop speaking of the "city" (which they destroyed) and instead to talk of the "urban," should compel them also to drop "country" (since it no longer exists). The uprooted and stressed-out masses are instead shown a countryside, a vision of the past that's easy to stage now that the country folk have been so depleted. It is a marketing campaign deployed on a "territory" in which everything must be valorized or reconstituted as national heritage. Everywhere it's the same chilling void, reaching into even the most remote and rustic corners.

The metropolis is this simultaneous death of city and country. It is the crossroads where all the petty bourgeois come together, in the middle of this middle class that stretches out indefinitely, as much a result of rural flight as of urban sprawl. To cover the planet with glass would fit perfectly the cynicism of contemporary architecture. A school, a hospital, or a media center are all variations on the same theme: transparency, neutrality, uniformity. These massive, fluid buildings are conceived without any need to know what they will house. They *could be here* as much as anywhere else. What to do with all the office towers at La Défense in Paris, the apartment blocks of Lyon's La Part Dieu, or the shopping complexes of EuraLille? The expression "*flambant neuf*"[1] perfectly captures their destiny. A Scottish traveler testifies to the unique attraction of the power of fire, speaking after rebels had burned the Hôtel de Ville in Paris in May, 1871: "Never could I have imagined anything so beautiful. It's superb. I won't deny that the people of the Commune are frightful rogues. But what artists! And they were not even aware of their own masterpiece! [...] I have seen the ruins of Amalfi bathed in the azure swells of the Mediterranean, and the ruins of the Tung-hoor temples in Punjab. I've seen Rome and many other things. But nothing can compare to what I feasted my eyes on tonight."

There still remain some fragments of the city and some traces of the country caught up in the metropolitan mesh. But vitality has taken up quarters in the so-called "problem" neighborhoods. It's a paradox that the places thought to be the most uninhabitable turn out to be the only ones still in some way inhabited. An old squatted shack still feels more lived in than the so-called luxury apartments where it is only possible to set down the furniture and get the décor just right while waiting for the next move. Within many of today's megalopolises, the shantytowns are the last living and livable areas, and

---

1. "*flambant neuf*"—literally, "flaming new"—is the French equivalent of the English "brand new."

also, of course, the most deadly. They are the flip-side of the electronic décor of the global metropolis. The dormitory towers in the suburbs north of Paris, abandoned by a petty bourgeoisie that went off hunting for swimming pools, have been brought back to life by mass unemployment and now radiate more energy than the Latin Quarter. In words as much as fire.

The conflagration of November 2005 was not a result of extreme dispossession, as it is often por-trayed. It was, on the contrary, a complete possession of a territory. People can burn cars because they are pissed off, but to keep the riots going for a month, while keeping the police in check—to do that you have to know how to organize, you have to establish complicities, you have to know the terrain perfectly, and share a common language and a common enemy. Mile after mile and week after week, the fire spread. New blazes responded to the original ones, appearing where they were least expected. The grapevine can't be wiretapped.

The metropolis is a terrain of constant low-intensity conflict, in which the taking of Basra, Mogadishu, or Nablus mark points of culmination. For a long time, the city was a place for the military to avoid, or if anything, to besiege; but the metropolis is perfectly compatible with war. Armed conflict is only a moment in its constant reconfiguration. The battles conducted by the great powers resemble a kind of never-ending police campaign in the black holes of the metropolis, "whether in Burkina Faso, in the South Bronx, in Kamagasaki, in Chiapas, or in La Courneuve." No longer undertaken in view of victory or peace, or even the re-establishment of order, such "interventions" continue a security operation that is always already in progress. War is no longer a distinct event in time, but instead diffracts into a series of micro-operations, by both military and police, to ensure security.

The police and the army are evolving in parallel and in lock-step. A criminologist requests that the national riot police reorganize itself into small, pro-fessionalized, mobile units. The military academy, cradle of disciplinary methods, is rethinking its own hierarchical organization. For his infantry battalion a NATO officer employs a "participatory method that involves everyone in the analysis, preparation, execution, and evaluation of an action. The plan is considered and reconsidered for days, right through the training phase and according to the latest intel-ligence [...] There is nothing like group planning for building team cohesion and morale."

The armed forces don't simply adapt themselves to the metropolis, they produce it. Thus, since the battle of Nablus, Israeli soldiers have become interior designers. Forced by Palestinian guerrillas to aban-don the streets, which had become too dangerous, they learned to advance vertically and horizontally into the heart of the urban architecture, poking holes in walls and ceilings in order to move through them. An officer in the Israel Defense Forces, and a graduate in philosophy, explains: "the enemy interprets space in a traditional, classical manner, and I do not want to obey this interpretation and fall into his traps. [...] I want to surprise him! This is the essence of war. I need to win [...] This is why we opted for the methodology of moving through walls [...] Like a worm that eats its way forward." Urban space is more than just the theater of confrontation, it is also the means. This echoes the advice of Blanqui who recommended (in this case for the party of insurrection) that the future insurgents of Paris take over the houses on the barricaded streets to protect their positions, that they should bore holes in the walls to allow passage between houses, break down the ground floor stairwells and poke holes in the ceilings to defend themselves against potential attackers, rip out the doors and use them to barricade the windows, and turn each floor into a gun turret.

The metropolis is not just this urban pile-up, this final collision between city and country. It is also a flow of beings and things, a *current* that runs through fiber-optic networks, through high-speed train lines, satellites, and video surveillance cameras, making sure that this world keeps running straight to its ruin. It is a current that would like to drag everything along in its hopeless mobility, to *mobilize* each and every one of us. Where information pummels us like some kind of hostile force. Where the only thing left to do is run. Where it becomes hard to wait, even for the umpteenth subway train.

With the proliferation of means of movement and communication, and with the lure of always being elsewhere, we are continuously torn from the *here* and *now*. Hop on an intercity or commuter train, pick up a telephone—in order to be *already gone*. Such mobility only ever means uprootedness, isolation, exile. It would be insufferable if it weren't always the mobility *of a private space*, of a portable interior. The private bubble doesn't burst, it floats around. The process of cocooning is not going away, it is merely being put into motion. From a train station, to an office park, to a commercial bank, from one hotel to another, there is everywhere a foreignness, a feeling so banal and so habitual it becomes the last form of familiarity. Metropolitan excess is this capricious mixing of definite moods, indefinitely recombined. The city centers of the metropolis are not clones of themselves, but offer instead their own auras; we glide from one to the next, selecting this one and rejecting that one, to the tune of a kind of existential shopping trip among different styles of bars, people, designs, or playlists. "With my mp3 player, I'm the master of my world." To cope with the uniformity that surrounds us, our only option is to constantly renovate our own interior world, like a child who constructs the same little house over and over again, or like Robinson Crusoe reproducing his shopkeeper's universe on a desert island—yet our desert island is civilization itself, and there are billions of us continually washing up on it.

It is precisely due to this architecture of flows that the metropolis is one of the most vulnerable human arrangements that has ever existed. Supple, subtle, but vulnerable. A brutal shutting down of borders to fend off a raging epidemic, a sudden interruption of supply lines, organized blockades of the axes of communication—and the whole facade crumbles, a facade that can no longer mask the scenes of carnage haunting it from morning to night. The world would not be moving so fast if it didn't have to constantly outrun its own collapse.

The metropolis aims to shelter itself from inevitable malfunction via its network structure, via its entire technological infrastructure of nodes and connections, its decentralized architecture. The internet is said to be capable of surviving a nuclear attack. Permanent control of the flow of information, people and products makes the mobility of the metropolis secure, while its' tracking systems ensure that no shipping containers get lost, that not a single dollar is stolen in any transaction, and that no terrorist ends up on an airplane. Thanks to an RFID chip, a biometric passport, a DNA profile.

But the metropolis also produces the means of its own destruction. An American security expert explains the defeat in Iraq as a result of the guerrillas' ability to take advantage of new ways of communicating. The US invasion didn't so much import democracy to Iraq as it did cybernetic networks. They brought with them one of the weapons of their own defeat. The proliferation of mobile phones and internet access points gave the guerrillas newfound ways to self-organize, and allowed them to become such elusive targets.

Every network has its weak points, the nodes that must be undone in order to interrupt circulation, to unwind the web. The last great European electrical blackout proved it: a single incident with a high-voltage wire and a good part of the continent was plunged into darkness. In order for something to rise up in the midst of the metropolis and open up other possibilities, the first act must be to interrupt its *perpetuum mobile*. That is what the Thai rebels understood when they knocked out electrical stations. That is what the French anti-CPE[2] protestors

2. A 2006 movement in France, principally of university and high-school students, against a new employment law (*Contrat première embauche*—CPE) permitting less secure job contracts for young people.

understood in 2006 when they shut down the universities with a view toward shutting down the entire economy. That is what the American longshoremen understood when they struck in October 2002 in support of three hundred jobs, blocking the main ports on the West Coast for ten days. The American economy is so dependent on goods coming from Asia that the cost of the blockade was over a billion dollars per day. With ten thousand people, the largest economic power in the world can be brought to its knees. According to certain "experts," if the action had lasted another month, it would have produced "a recession in the United States and an economic nightmare in Southeast Asia."

Fifth Circle

"FEWER POSSESSIONS, MORE CONNECTIONS!"

Thirty years of "crisis," mass unemployment and flagging growth, and they still want us to believe in the economy. Thirty years punctuated, it is true, by delusionary interludes: the interlude of 1981–83, when we were deluded into thinking a government of the left might make people better off; the "easy money" interlude of 1986–89, when we were all supposed to be playing the market and getting rich; the internet interlude of 1998–2001, when everyone was going to get a virtual career through being well-connected, when a diverse but united France, cultured and multicultural, would bring home every World Cup. But here we are, we've drained our supply of delusions, we've hit rock bottom and are totally broke, or buried in debt.

We have to see that the economy is not "in" crisis, the economy is itself the crisis. It's not that there's not enough work, it's that there is *too much of it*. All things considered, it's not the crisis that depresses us, it's growth. We must admit that the litany of stock market prices moves us about as much as a Latin mass. Luckily for us, there are quite a few of us who have come to this conclusion. We're not talking about those who live off various scams, who deal in this or that, or who have been on welfare for the last ten years. Or of all those who no longer find their identity in their jobs and live for their time off. Nor are we talking about those who've been swept under the rug, the hidden ones who make do with the least, and yet outnumber the rest. All those struck by this strange *mass detachment*, adding to the ranks of retirees and the cynically overexploited flexible labor force. We're not talking about them, although they too should, in one way or another, arrive at a similar conclusion.

We are talking about all of the countries, indeed entire continents, that have lost faith in the economy, either because they've seen the IMF come and go amid crashes and enormous losses, or because they've gotten a taste of the World Bank. The soft crisis of vocation that the West is now experiencing is completely absent in these places. What is happening in Guinea, Russia, Argentina and Bolivia is a violent and long-lasting debunking of this religion and its clergy. "What do you call a thousand IMF economists lying at the bottom of the sea?" went the joke at the World Bank—"a good start." A Russian joke: "Two economists meet. One asks the other: 'You understand what's happening?' The other responds: 'Wait, I'll explain it to you.' 'No, no,' says the first, 'explaining is no problem, I'm an economist, too. What I'm asking is: do you understand it?" Entire sections of this clergy pretend to be dissidents and to critique this religion's dogma. The latest attempt to revive the so-called "science of the economy"—a current that straight-facedly refers to itself as "post autistic economics"—makes a living from dismantling the usurpations, sleights of hand and cooked books of a science whose only tangible function is to rattle the monstrance during the vociferations of the chiefs, giving their demands for submission a bit of ceremony, and ultimately doing what religions have always done: *providing explanations*. For the general misery becomes intolerable the moment it is shown for what it is, a thing without cause or reason.

Nobody respects money anymore, neither those who have it nor those who don't. When asked what they want to be some day, twenty percent of young Germans answer "artist." Work is no longer endured as a given of the human condition. The accounting departments of corporations confess that they have no idea where value comes from. The market's bad reputation would have done it in a decade ago if not for the bluster and fury, not to mention the deep pockets, of its apologists. It is common sense now to see progress as synonymous with disaster. In the world of the economic, everything is in flight, just like in the USSR under Andropov.[1] Anyone who has spent

---

1. Andropov was General Secretary of the Communist Party of the Soviet Union from 1982 to 1984.

a little time analyzing the final years of the USSR knows very well that the pleas for goodwill coming from our rulers, all of their fantasies about some future that has disappeared without a trace, all of their professions of faith in "reforming" this and that, are just the first fissures in the structure of the wall. The collapse of the socialist bloc was in no way a victory of capitalism; it was merely the breakdown of one of the forms capitalism takes. Besides, the demise of the USSR did not come about because a people revolted, but because the nomenklatura was undergoing a changeover. When it proclaimed the end of socialism, a small fraction of the ruling class emancipated itself from the anachronistic duties that still bound it to the people. It took *private* control of what it already controlled in the name of "everyone." In the factories, the joke went: "We pretend to work, and they pretend to pay us." The oligarchy replied, "There's no point, let's stop pretending!" They ended up with the raw materials, industrial infrastructures, the military-industrial complex, the banks and the nightclubs. Everyone else got poverty or emigration. Just as no one in Andropov's time believed in the USSR, no one in the meeting halls, workshops and offices believes in France today. "There's no point," respond the bosses and political leaders, who no longer even bother to smooth the edges of the "iron laws of the economy." They strip factories in the middle of the night and announce the shutdown early next morning. They no longer hesitate to send in anti-terrorism units to shut down a strike, as was done with the ferries and the occupied recycling center in Rennes. The brutal activity of power today consists both in administering this ruin while at the same time establishing the framework for a "new economy."

And yet we had gotten used to the economy. For generations we were disciplined, pacified and made into *subjects*, productive by nature and content to consume. And suddenly everything that we were determined to forget is revealed: that *the economy is political*. And that this politics is, today, a politics of selection within a humanity that has, largely become superfluous. From Colbert[2] to de Gaulle, by way of Napoleon III, the state has always treated the economic as political, as have the bourgeoisie (who profit from it) and the proletariat (who confront it). All that's left is this strange, middling part of the population, the curious and powerless aggregate *of those who take no sides*: the petty bourgeoisie. They have always pretended to believe in the economy as a reality—because their neutrality is safe there. Small business owners, small bosses, minor bureaucrats, managers, professors, journalists, middlemen of every sort make up this non-class in France, this

2. Jean-Baptiste Colbert served as the French minister of finance from 1665 to 1683 under Louis XIV.

social gelatin composed of the mass of all those who just want to live their little private lives at a distance from history and its tumults. This swamp is predisposed to be the champion of false consciousness, half-asleep and always ready to close its eyes on the war that rages all around it. Each clarification of a front in this war is thus accompanied in France by the invention of some new fad. For the past ten years, it was ATTAC[3] and its improbable Tobin tax —a tax whose implementation would require nothing less than a global government—with its sympathy for the "real economy" as opposed to the financial markets, not to mention its touching nostalgia for the state. The comedy lasts only so long before turning into a masquerade. And then another fad replaces it. So now we have *"negative growth."*[4] Whereas ATTAC tried to save economics *as a science* with its popular education courses, negative growth would preserve it *as a morality*. There is only one alternative to the coming apocalypse: reduce growth. Consume and produce

---

3. Association for the Taxation of Financial Transactions for the Aid of Citizens (ATTAC) is a non-party political organization that advocates social-democratic reforms, particularly the "Tobin tax" on international foreign exchange intended to curtail currency speculation and fund social policies.

4. *La décroissance* (negative growth) is a French left–ecological movement which advocates a reduction in consumption and production for the sake of environmental sustainability and an improvement in the quality of life.

less. Become joyously frugal. Eat organic, ride your bike, stop smoking, and pay close attention to the products you buy. Be content with what's strictly necessary. Voluntary simplicity. "Rediscover true wealth in the blossoming of convivial social relations in a healthy world." "Don't use up our natural capital." Work toward a "healthy economy." "No regulation through chaos." "Avoid a social crisis that would threaten democracy and humanism." Simply put: *become economical.* Go back to daddy's economy, to the golden age of the petty bourgeoisie: the '50s. "When an individual is frugal, property serves its function perfectly, which is to allow the individual to enjoy his or her own life sheltered from public existence, in the private sanctuary of his or her life."

A graphic designer wearing a handmade sweater is drinking a fruity cocktail with some friends on the terrace of an "ethnic" café. They're chatty and cordial, they joke around a bit, they make sure not to be too loud or too quiet, they smile at each other, a little blissfully: we are so civilized. Afterwards, some of them will go work in the neighborhood community garden, while others will dabble in pottery, some Zen Buddhism, or in the making of an animated film. They find communion in the smug feeling that they constitute a new humanity, wiser and more refined than the previous one. And they are right. There is a curious agreement between

Apple and the negative growth movement about the civilization of the future. Some people's idea of returning to the economy of yesteryear offers others the convenient screen behind which a great technological leap forward can be launched. For in history there is no going back. Any exhortation to return to the past is only the expression of one form of consciousness of the present, and rarely the least modern. It is not by chance that negative growth is the banner of the dissident advertisers of the magazine *Casseurs de Pub*.[5] The inventors of zero growth—the Club of Rome in 1972—were themselves a group of industrialists and bureaucrats who relied on a research paper written by cyberneticians at MIT.

This convergence is hardly a coincidence. It is part of the forced march towards a modernized economy. Capitalism got as much as it could from undoing all the old social ties, and it is now in the process of remaking itself by rebuilding these same ties *on its own terms*. Contemporary metropolitan social life is its incubator. In the same way, it ravaged the natural world and is now taken with the crazy notion of reconstituting nature as so many controlled environments, furnished with all the necessary sensors. This new humanity requires a new economy that would no longer be a separate sphere of existence but, rather, its very tissue, the raw

---

5. A French equivalent of the magazine *Adbusters*.

material of human relations. It requires a new definition of work as work on oneself, a new definition of capital as human capital, a new idea of production as the production of relations, and consumption as the consumption of situations; and above all a new idea of value that would encompass all of the qualities of beings. This burgeoning "bioeconomy" conceives the planet as a closed system to be managed and claims to establish the foundations for a science that would integrate all the parameters of life. Such a science could make us miss the good old days when unreliable indices like GDP growth were supposed to measure the well-being of a people, but at least no one believed in them.

"Revalorize the non-economic aspects of life" is the slogan shared by the negative growth movement and by capital's reform program. Eco-villages, video-surveillance cameras, spirituality, biotechnologies and sociability all belong to the same "civilizational paradigm" now taking shape, that of a total economy rebuilt from the ground up. Its intellectual matrix is none other than cybernetics, the science of systems—that is, the science *of their control*. In the 17th century, in order to impose the economic system and its ethos of work and greed in a definitive way, it was necessary to confine and eliminate the whole seamy mass of layabouts, liars, witches, madmen, scoundrels and all the other vagrant poor, a whole humanity whose very existence gave the lie to the order of interest and restraint. The new economy cannot be established without a similar selection of subjects and zones singled out for transformation. The chaos that we constantly hear about will either provide the opportunity for this selection, or for our victory over this odious project.

Sixth Circle

"THE ENVIRONMENT IS AN INDUSTRIAL CHALLENGE"

Ecology is the discovery of the decade. For the last thirty years we've left it up to the environmentalists, joking about it on Sunday so that we can act concerned again on Monday. And now it's caught up to us, invading the airwaves like a hit song in summertime, because it's 68 degrees in December.

One quarter of the fish species have disappeared from the ocean. The rest won't last much longer.

Bird flu alert: we are given assurances that hundreds of thousands of migrating birds will be shot from the sky.

Mercury levels in human breast milk are ten times higher than the legal level for cows. And these lips which swell up after I bite the apple—but it came from the farmer's market. The simplest gestures have become toxic. One dies at the age of 35 from "a prolonged illness" that's to be managed just like one manages everything else. We should've seen it coming before we got to this place, to ward B of the palliative care center.

We have to admit it: this whole "catastrophe," which they so noisily inform us about, doesn't really touch us. At least not until we are hit by one of its foreseeable consequences. It may concern us, but it doesn't touch us. And that is the real catastrophe.

There is no "environmental catastrophe." The catastrophe is the *environment itself.* The environment is what's left to man after he's lost everything. Those who live in a neighborhood, a street, a valley, a war zone, a workshop—they don't have an "environment;" they move through a *world* peopled by presences, dangers, friends, enemies, moments of life and death, all kinds of beings. Such a world has its own consistency, which varies according to the intensity and quality of the ties attaching us to all of these beings, to all of these places. It's only we, the children of the final dispossession, exiles of the final hour—who come into the world in concrete cubes, pick our fruits at the supermarket, and watch for an echo of the world on television—only we get to *have an environment.* And there's no one but us to witness our own annihilation, as if it were just a simple change of scenery, to get indignant about the latest progress of the disaster, to patiently compile its encyclopedia.

What has congealed as an environment is a relationship to the world based on management, which is to say, on estrangement. A relationship to the world wherein we're not made up *just as much* of the rustling trees, the smell of frying oil in the building, running water, the hubbub of schoolrooms, the mugginess of summer evenings. A relationship to the world where there is me and then my environment, surrounding me but never really constituting me. We have become neighbors in a planetary board meeting. It's difficult to imagine a more complete hell.

No material habitat has ever deserved the name "environment," except perhaps the metropolis of today. The digitized voices making announcements, streetcars with such a 21st century whistle, bluish streetlamps shaped like giant matchsticks, pedestrians done up like failed fashion models, the silent rotation of a video surveillance camera, the lucid clicking of the subway turnstyles, supermarket checkouts, office time-clocks, the electronic ambiance of the cybercafé, the profusion of plasma screens, express lanes and latex. Never has a setting been so able to do without the souls traversing it. Never has a milieu been more automatic. Never has a context been so indifferent, and demanded in return—as the price of survival—such an equal indifference from us. Ultimately the environment is nothing more than the relationship to the world that is proper to the metropolis, and that projects itself onto everything that would escape it.

The situation is like this: they hired our parents to destroy this world, and now they'd like to put us to work rebuilding it, and—to add insult to injury—at a profit. The morbid excitement that animates journalists and advertisers these days as they report each new proof of global warming reveals the steely smile of the new green capitalism, in the making since the '70s, which we expected at the turn of the century but which never came. Well, here it is! It's sustainability! Alternative solutions, that's it too! The health of the planet demands it! No doubt about it anymore, it's a green scene; the environment will be the pivot of the 21st century political economy. A new volley of "industrial solutions" comes with each new catastrophic possibility.

The inventor of the H-bomb, Edward Teller, proposes shooting millions of tons of metallic dust into the stratosphere to stop global warming. NASA, frustrated at having to shelve its idea of an anti-missile shield in the museum of cold war horrors, suggests installing a gigantic mirror beyond the moon's orbit to protect us from the sun's now-fatal rays. Another vision of the future: a motorized humanity, driving on bio-ethanol from Sao Paulo to Stockholm; the dream of cereal growers the world over, for it only means converting *all* of the planet's arable lands into soy and sugar beet fields. Eco-friendly cars, clean energy, and environmental consulting coexist painlessly with the latest Chanel ad in the pages of glossy magazines.

We are told that the environment has the incomparable merit of being the first truly *global problem* presented to humanity. A *global problem*, which is to say a problem that only those who are organized on a global level will be able to solve. And we know who they are. These are the very same groups that for close to a century have been the vanguard of disaster, and certainly intend to remain so, for the small price of a change of logo. That EDF[1] had the impudence to trot out its nuclear program as the *new solution* to the global energy crisis goes to show how much the new solutions resemble the old problems.

From Secretaries of State to the backrooms of alternative cafés, concerns are always expressed in the same words, the same as they've always been. We have to get *mobilized*. This time it's not to rebuild the country like in the post-war era, not for the Ethiopians like in the '80s, not for employment like in the '90s. No, this time it's for the environment. It thanks you for your participation. Al Gore and negative growth movement stand side by side with the eternal great souls of the Republic to do their part in reinvigorating the little people of the Left and the well-known idealism of youth. Voluntary austerity writ large on their banner, they work benevolently to get us ready for the "coming ecological state of

---

1. Électricité de France (EDF) is the main electricity generation and distribution company in France and one of the largest in the world, supplying most of its power from nuclear reactors.

emergency." The globular sticky mass of their guilt lands on our tired shoulders, pressuring us to cultivate our garden, sort out our trash, and eco-compost the leftovers of this macabre feast.

Managing the phasing out of nuclear power, excess CO_2 in the atmosphere, melting glaciers, hurricanes, epidemics, global overpopulation, erosion of the soil, mass extinction of living species... this will be our burden. They tell us, "everyone must do their part," if we want to save our beautiful model of civilization. We have to consume a little less *to be able to keep consuming*. We have to produce organically *to keep producing*. We have to control ourselves *to go on controlling*. This is the logic of a world straining to maintain itself while giving itself an air of historical rupture. This is how they would like to convince us to participate in the great industrial challenges of this century. And in our bewilderment we're ready to leap into the arms of the very same ones who presided over the devastation, in the hope that they will get us out of it.

Ecology isn't simply the logic of a total economy; it's the new morality of capital. The system's internal state of crisis and the rigorous screening that's underway demand a new criterion in the name of which this screening and selection will be carried out. From one era to the next, the idea of virtue has never been anything but an invention of vice. Without ecology, how could we justify the existence of two different diets, one "healthy and organic" for the rich and their children, and the other notoriously toxic for the plebes, whose offspring are damned to obesity. The planetary hyper-bourgeoisie wouldn't be able to make its normal lifestyle seem respectable if its latest whims weren't so scrupulously "respectful of the environment." Without ecology, nothing would have enough authority to gag every objection to the exorbitant progress of control.

Tracking, transparency, certification, eco-taxes, environmental excellence, and the policing of water, all give us an idea of the coming state of ecological emergency. Everything is permitted to a power structure that bases its authority in Nature, in health and in well-being.

"Once the new economic and behavioral culture has become common practice, coercive measures will *doubtless* fall into disuse of their own accord." You'd have to have all the ridiculous aplomb of a TV crusader to maintain such a frozen perspective and in the same breath incite us to feel sufficiently "sorry for the planet" to get mobilized, while remaining anesthetized enough to watch the whole thing with restraint and civility. The new green asceticism is precisely the *self-control* that is required of us all in order to negotiate a rescue operation where the system has taken itself hostage. Henceforth, it's in the name of environmentalism that we must all tighten our belts, just as we did yesterday in the name of the economy. The roads could certainly be transformed into bicycle paths, we ourselves could perhaps, to a certain degree, be grateful one day for a guaranteed income, but only at the price of an entirely therapeutic existence. Those who claim that generalized self-control will spare us from an environmental dictatorship are lying: the one will prepare the way for the other, and we'll end up with both.

As long as there is Man and Environment, the police will be there between them.

Everything about the environmentalists' discourse must be turned upside-down. Where they talk of "catastrophes" to label the present system's mismanagement of beings and things, we only see the catastrophe of its all too perfect operation. The greatest wave of famine ever known in the tropics (1876-1879) coincided with a global drought, but more significantly, it also coincided with the apogee of colonization. The destruction of the peasant's world and of local alimentary practices meant the disappearance of the means for dealing with scarcity. More than the lack of water, it was the effect of the rapidly expanding colonial economy that littered the Tropics with millions of emaciated corpses. What is presented everywhere as an ecological catastrophe has never stopped being, above all, the manifestation of a disastrous relationship to the world. Inhabiting a nowhere makes us vulnerable to the slightest jolt in the system, to the slightest climactic risk. As the latest tsunami approached and the tourists continued to frolic in the waves, the islands' hunter-gatherers rushed away from the coast, following the birds. Environmentalism's present paradox is that under the pretext of saving the planet from desolation it merely saves the causes of its desolation.

The normal functioning of the world serves to hide our state of truly catastrophic dispossession. What is called "catastrophe" is no more than the forced suspension of this state, one of those rare moments when we regain some sort of presence in the world. Let the petroleum reserves run out earlier than expected; let the international flows that regulate the tempo of the metropolis be interrupted; let us suffer some great social disruption and some great "return to savagery of the population," a "planetary threat," the "end of civilization!" Whatever. Any loss of control would be preferable to all the crisis management scenarios they envision. When this comes, the specialists in sustainable development won't be the ones with the best advice. It's within the malfunction and short-circuits of the system that we find the elements of a response whose logic would be to abolish the problems themselves. Among the signatory nations to the Kyoto Protocol, the only countries that have fulfilled their commitments, in spite of themselves, are Ukraine and Romania.

Guess why. The most advanced experimentation with "organic" agriculture on a global level has taken place since 1989 on the island of Cuba. Guess why. And it's along the African highways, and nowhere else, that auto mechanics has been elevated to a form of popular art. Guess how.

What makes the crisis desirable is that in the crisis the environment ceases to be the environment. We are forced to reestablish contact, albeit a potentially fatal one, with what's there, to rediscover the rhythms of reality. What surrounds us is no longer a landscape, a panorama, a theater, but something to inhabit, something we need to come to terms with, something we can learn from. We won't let ourselves be led astray by the ones who've brought about the the "catastrophe." Where the managers platonically discuss among themselves how they might decrease emissions "without breaking the bank," the only realistic option we can see is to "break the bank" as soon as possible and, in the meantime, take advantage of every collapse in the system to increase our own strength.

New Orleans, a few days after Hurricane Katrina. In this apocalyptic atmosphere, here and there, life is reorganizing itself. In the face of the inaction of the public authorities, who were too busy cleaning up the tourist areas of the French Quarter and protecting shops to help the poorer city dwellers, forgotten forms are reborn. In spite of occasionally strong-armed attempts to evacuate the area, in spite of white supremacist lynch mobs, a lot of people refused to leave the terrain. For the latter, who refused to be deported like "environmental refugees" all over the country, and for those who came from all around to join them in solidarity, responding to a call from a former Black Panther, self-organization came back to the fore. In a few weeks time, the Common Ground Clinic was set up.[2] From the very first days, this veritable "country hospital" provided free and effective treatment to those who needed it, thanks to the constant influx of volunteers. For more than a year now, the clinic is still the base of a daily resistance to the clean-sweep operation of government bulldozers, which are trying to turn that part of the city into a pasture for property developers. Popular kitchens, supplies, street medicine, illegal takeovers, the construction of emergency housing, all this practical knowledge accumulated here and there in the course

---

2. A certain distance leads to a certain obscurity. Common Ground has been criticized in North America for the fact that its activities were geared towards a return to normality—that is, to the normal functioning of things. In any case it clearly remains in the realm of classical politics. The founder of Common Ground, former Black Panther Malik Rahim, eventually used the project as part of his unsuccessful run for the US Congress in 2008. It was later revealed that one of the main spokesmen for the project, Brandon Darby, was an FBI informant.

of a life, has now found a space where it can be deployed. Far from the uniforms and sirens.

Whoever knew the penniless joy of these New Orleans neighborhoods before the catastrophe, their defiance towards the state and the widespread practice of making do with what's available wouldn't be at all surprised by what became possible there. On the other hand, anyone trapped in the anemic and atomized everyday routine of our residential deserts might doubt that such determination could be found anywhere anymore. Reconnecting with such gestures, buried under years of normalized life, is the only practicable means of not sinking down with the world, while we dream of an age that is equal to our passions.

"WE ARE BUILDING A CIVILIZED SPACE HERE"

The first global slaughter, which from 1914 to 1918 did away with a large portion of the urban and rural proletariat, was waged in the name of freedom, democracy, and civilization. For the past five years, the so-called "war on terror" with its special operations and targeted assassinations has been pursued in the name of these same values. Yet the resemblance stops there: at the level of appearances. The value of civilization is no longer so obvious that it can be brought to the natives as a package. Freedom is no longer a name scrawled on walls, for today it is always followed, as if by its shadow, with the word "security." And it is well known that democracy can be dissolved in pure and simple "emergency" edicts—for example, in the official reinstitution of torture in the US, or in France's Perben II law.[1]

In a single century, freedom, democracy and civilization have reverted to the state of hypotheses. The leaders' work from now on consists in shaping

---

1. Perben II is a law introduced in France in 2004 that targets "organized crime" and "delinquency" and allows for sentencing without trial.

the material and moral as well as symbolic and social conditions in which these hypotheses can be more or less validated, in configuring spaces where they can seem to function. All means to these ends are acceptable, even the least democratic, the least civilized, the most repressive. It was a century in which democracy regularly presided over the birth of fascist regimes, civilization constantly rhymed—to the tune of Wagner or Iron Maiden—with extermination, and in which, one day in 1929, freedom showed its two faces: a banker throwing himself from a window and a family of workers dying of hunger. Since then—let's say, since 1945—it's taken for granted that manipulating the masses, secret service operations, the restriction of public liberties, and the complete sovereignty of a wide array of police forces were appropriate ways to ensure democracy, freedom and civilization. At the final stage of this evolution, we see the first socialist mayor of Paris putting the finishing touches on urban pacification with a new police protocol for a poor neighborhood, announced with the following carefully chosen words: "We're building a civilized space here." There's nothing more to say, everything has to be destroyed.

Though it seems general in nature, the question of civilization is not at all a philosophical one. A civilization is not an abstraction hovering over life. It is what rules, takes possession of, colonizes the most banal, personal, daily existence. It's what holds together that which is most intimate and most general. In France, civilization is inseparable from the state. The older and more powerful the state, the less it is a super-structure or exoskeleton of a society and the more it constitutes the subjectivities that people it. The French state is the very texture of French subjectivities, the form assumed by the centuries-old castration of its subjects. Thus it should come as no surprise that in their deliriums psychiatric patients are always confusing themselves with political figures, that we agree that our leaders are the root of all our ills, that we like to grumble so much about them and that this grumbling is the consecration that crowns them as our masters. Here, politics is not considered something outside of us but part of ourselves. The life we invest in these figures is the same life that's taken from us.

If there is a French exception, this is why. Every-thing, even the global influence of French literature, is a result of this amputation. In France, literature is the prescribed space for the amusement of the castrated. It is the formal freedom conceded to those who cannot accommodate themselves to the noth-ingness of their real freedom. That's what accounts for all the obscene winks exchanged, for centuries now, between the statesmen and men of letters in this country, as each gladly dons the other's costume. That's also why intellectuals here tend to talk so loud when they're so meek, and why they always fail at the decisive moment, the only moment that would've given meaning to their existence, but that also would've had them banished from their profession.

There exists a credible thesis that modern literature was born with Baudelaire, Heine, and Flaubert as a repercussion of the state massacre of June 1848. It's in the blood of the Parisian insurgents, against the silence surrounding the slaughter, that modern literary forms were born—spleen, ambivalence, fetishism of form, and morbid detachment. The neurotic affection that the French pledge to their Republic—in the name of which every smudge of ink assumes an air of dignity, and any pathetic hack is honored—underwrites the perpetual repression of its originary sacrifices. The June days of 1848— 1,500 dead in combat, thousands of summary executions of prisoners, and the Assembly welcoming the surrender of the last barricade with cries of "Long Live the Republic!"—and the Bloody Week of 1871 are birthmarks no surgery can hide.

In 1945, Kojeve wrote: "The "official" political ideal of France and of the French is today still that of the nation-State, of the 'one and indivisible Republic.' On the other hand, in the depths of its soul, the country understands the inadequacy of this ideal, of the political anachronism of the strictly "national" idea. This feeling has admittedly not yet reached the level of a clear and distinct idea: The country cannot, and will not yet express it openly. Moreover, for the very reason of the unparalleled brilliance of its *national* past, it is especially difficult for France to recognize clearly and to accept frankly the fact of the end of the 'national' period of History and to understand all of its consequences. It is hard for a country which created, out of nothing, the ideological framework of nationalism and exported it to the whole world to recognize that all that remains of it now is a document to be filed in the historical archives."

This question of the nation-state and its mourning is at the heart of what for the past half-century can only be called *the French malaise*. We politely give the name of "alternation" to this twitchy indecision, this pendulum-like oscillation from left to right, then right to left; like a manic phase after a depressive one that is then followed by another, or the way a completely rhetorical critique of individualism uneasily co-exists with the most ferocious cynicism, or the greatest generosity with an aversion to crowds. Since 1945, this malaise, which seems to have dissipated only during the insurrectionary fervor of May 68, has continually worsened. The era of states, nations and republics is coming to an end, and the country that sacrificed all its vitality to these forms remains stunned by that fact. The trouble caused by Jospin's simple sentence "The state can't do everything" allows us to imagine the reaction when it becomes clear that the state can no longer do anything at all.

The feeling that we've been tricked is like a wound that is becoming increasingly infected. It's the source of the latent rage that just about anything will set off these days. The fact that in this country the obituary of the age of nations has yet to be written is the key to the French anachronism, and to the revolutionary possibilities France still has in store.

Whatever their outcome may be, the role of the next presidential elections will be to signal the end of French illusions and to burst the historical bubble in which we are living—and which makes possible *events* like the anti-CPE movement, that was puzzled over by other countries as if it were some bad dream that escaped from the '70s. That's why, deep down, no one wants these elections. France is indeed the *red* lantern of the western zone.[2]

Today the West is the GI who dashes into Fallujah on an M1 Abrams tank, listening to heavy metal at top volume. It's the tourist lost on the Mongolian plains, mocked by all, who clutches his credit card as his only lifeline. It's the CEO who swears by the game Go. It's the young girl who looks for happiness in clothes, guys, and moisturizing creams. It's the Swiss human rights activist who travels to the four corners of the earth to show solidarity with all the world's rebels—provided they've been defeated. It's the

2. The "red lantern" is the last place finisher in the Tour de France.

Spaniard who could care less about political freedom now that he's been granted sexual freedom. It's the art lover who wants us to be awestruck before the "modern genius" of a century of artists, from surrealism to Viennese actionism, all competing to see who could best spit in the face of civilization. It's the cyberneticist who's found a realistic theory of consciousness in Buddhism and the quantum physicist who's hoping that dabbling in Hindu metaphysics will inspire new scientific discoveries.

The West is a civilization that has survived all the prophecies of its collapse with a singular stratagem. Just as the bourgeoisie had to deny itself *as a class* in order to permit the bourgeoisification of society as a whole, from the worker to the baron; just as capital had to sacrifice itself *as a wage relation* in order to impose itself as a social relation—becoming cultural capital and health capital in addition to finance capital; just as Christianity had to sacrifice itself as a religion in order to survive as an affective structure— as a vague injunction to humility, compassion, and weakness; *so the West has sacrificed itself as a particular civilization in order to impose itself as a universal culture*. The operation can be summarized like this: an entity in its death throes sacrifices itself as a content in order to survive as a form.

The fragmented individual survives as a form thanks to the "spiritual" technologies of counseling. Patriarchy survives by attributing to women all the worst attributes of men: willfulness, self-control, insensitivity. A disintegrated society survives by propagating an epidemic of sociability and entertainment. So it goes with all the great, outmoded fictions of the West maintaining themselves through artifices that contradict these fictions point by point.

There is no "clash of civilizations." There is a clinically dead civilization kept alive by all sorts of life-support machines that spread a peculiar plague into the planet's atmosphere. At this point it can no longer believe in a single one of its own "values," and any affirmation of them is considered an impudent act, a provocation that should and must be taken apart, *deconstructed*, and returned to a state of doubt. Today Western imperialism is the imperialism of relativism, of the "It all depends on your point of view"; it's the eye-rolling or the wounded indignation at anyone who's stupid, primitive, or presumptuous enough to still believe in something, to affirm anything at all. You can see the dogmatism of constant questioning give its complicit wink of the eye everywhere in the universities and among the literary intelligentsias. No critique is too radical among postmodernist thinkers, as long as it maintains this total absence of certitude. A century ago, scandal was identified with any particularly unruly and raucous negation, while today it's found in any affirmation that fails to tremble.

No social order can base itself for long on the principle that nothing is true. Yet it must be *made secure*. Applying the concept of "security" to everything these days is the expression of a project to securely fasten onto places, behaviors, and even people themselves, an ideal order to which they are no longer ready to submit. Saying "nothing is true" says nothing about the world but everything about the Western concept of truth. For the West, truth is not an attribute of beings or things, but of their representation. A representation that conforms to experience is held to be true. Science is, in the last analysis, this empire of universal verification. Since all human behavior, from the most ordinary to the most learned, is based on a foundation of unevenly formulated facts, and since all practices start from a point where things and their representations can no longer be distinguished, a measure of truth that the Western concept excludes enters into every life. We talk in the West about "real people," but only in order to mock these simpletons. This is why Westerners have always been thought of as liars and hypocrites by the people they've colonized. This is why they're envied for what they *have*, for their technological development, but never for what they *are*, for which they are rightly held in contempt. Sade, Nietzsche and Artaud wouldn't be taught in schools if the kind of truth mentioned above was not discredited in advance. Containing all affirmations and deactivating all certainties as they irresistibly come to light—such is the long labor of the Western intellect. The police and philosophy are two convergent, if formally distinct, means to this end.

Of course, this imperialism of the relative finds a suitable enemy in every empty dogmatism, in whatever form of Marxist-Leninism, Salifism, or Neo-Nazism: anyone who, like Westerners, mistakes provocation for affirmation.

At this juncture, any strictly social contestation that refuses to see that what we're facing is not the crisis of a society but the extinction of a civilization becomes an accomplice in its perpetuation. It's even become a contemporary strategy to critique this society in the vain hope of saving the civilization.

So we have a corpse on our backs, but we won't be able to shake it off just like that. Nothing is to be expected from the end of civilization, from its clinical death. Such a thing can only be of interest to historians. It's a *fact*, and it must be translated into a *decision*. Facts can be conjured away, but decision is political. To decide for the death of civilization, then to work out *how* it will happen: only decision will rid us of the corpse.

GET GOING!

We can no longer even see how an insurrection might begin. Sixty years of pacification and containment of historical upheavals, sixty years of democratic anesthesia and the management of events, have dulled our perception of the real, our sense of the war in progress. We need to start by recovering this perception.

It's useless to get *indignant* about openly unconstitutional laws such as Perben II. It's futile to legally protest the complete implosion of the legal framework. We have to get organized.

It's useless to get *involved* in this or that citizens' group, in this or that dead-end of the far left, or in the latest "community effort." Every organization that claims to contest the present order mimics the form, mores and language of miniature states. Thus far, every impulse to "do politics differently" has only contributed to the indefinite spread of the state's tentacles.

It's useless to *react* to the news of the day; instead we should understand each report as a maneuver in a hostile field of strategies to be decoded, operations designed to provoke a specific reaction. It's these operations themselves that should be taken as the real information contained in these pieces of news.

It's useless *to wait*—for a breakthrough, for the revolution, the nuclear apocalypse or a social movement. To go on waiting is madness. The catastrophe is not coming, it is here. We are already situated *within* the collapse of a civilization. It is within this reality that we must choose sides.

To no longer wait is, in one way or another, to enter into the logic of insurrection. It is once again to hear the slight but always present trembling of terror in the voices of our leaders. Because governing has never been anything other than postponing by a thousand subterfuges the moment when the crowd will string you up, and every act of government is nothing but a way of not losing control of the population.

We're setting out from a point of extreme isolation, of extreme weakness. An insurrectional process must be built from the ground up. Nothing appears less likely than an insurrection, but nothing is more necessary.

FIND EACH OTHER

Attach yourself to what you feel to be true.
Begin there.

An encounter, a discovery, a vast wave of strikes, an earthquake: every event produces truth by changing our way of being in the world. Conversely, any observation that leaves us indifferent, doesn't affect us, doesn't commit us to anything, no longer deserves the name truth. There's a truth beneath every gesture, every practice, every relationship, and every situation. We usually just avoid it, *manage* it, which produces the madness of so many in our era. In reality, everything involves everything else. The feeling that one is living a lie is still a truth. It is a matter of not letting it go, of starting from there. A truth isn't a view on the world but what binds us to it in an irreducible way. A truth isn't something we hold but something that carries us. It makes and unmakes me, constitutes and undoes me as an individual; it distances me from many and brings me closer to those who also experience it. An isolated being who holds fast to a truth will inevitably meet others like her. In fact, every insurrectional process starts from a truth that we refuse to give up. During the '80s in Hamburg, a few inhabitants of a squatted house decided that from then on they would only be evicted over their dead bodies. A neighborhood was besieged by tanks and helicopters, with days of street battles, huge demonstrations—and a mayor who, finally, capitulated. In 1940, Georges Guingouin, the "first French resistance fighter," started with nothing but the certainty of his refusal of the Nazi occupation. At that time, to the Communist Party, he was nothing but a "madman living in the woods," until there were 20,000 madmen living in the woods, and Limoges was liberated.

Don't back away from what is political in friendship.

We've been given a neutral idea of friendship, understood as a pure affection with no consequences. But all affinity is affinity *within* a common truth. Every encounter is an encounter *within* a common affirmation, even the affirmation of destruction. No bonds are innocent in an age when holding onto something and refusing to let go usually leads to unemployment, where you have to lie to work, and you have to keep on working in order to continue lying. People who swear by quantum physics and pursue its consequences in all domains are no less bound politically than comrades fighting against a multinational agribusiness. They will all be led, sooner or later, to defection and to combat.

The pioneers of the workers' movement were able to find each other in the workshop, then in the factory. They had the strike to show their numbers and unmask the scabs. They had the wage relation, pitting the party of capital against the party of labor, on which they could draw the lines of solidarity and of battle on a global scale. We have the whole of social space in which to find each other. We have everyday insubordination for showing our numbers and unmasking cowards. We have our hostility to this civilization for drawing lines of solidarity and of battle on a global scale.

Expect nothing from organizations.
Beware of all existing social milieus,
and above all, don't become one.

It's not uncommon, in the course of a significant breaking of the social bond, to cross paths with organizations—political, labor, humanitarian, community associations, etc. Among their members, one may even find individuals who are sincere—if a little desperate—who are enthusiastic—if a little conniving. Organizations are attractive due to their apparent consistency—they have a history, a head office, a name, resources, a leader, a strategy and a discourse. They are nonetheless empty structures, which, in spite of their grand origins, can never be filled. In all their affairs, at every level, these organizations are concerned above all with their own survival as organizations, and little else. Their repeated betrayals have often alienated the commitment of their own rank and file. And this is why you can, on occasion, run into worthy beings within them. But the promise of the encounter can only be realized outside the organization and, unavoidably, at odds with it.

Far more dreadful are *social milieus*, with their supple texture, their gossip, and their informal hierarchies. Flee all milieus. Each and every milieu is oriented towards the neutralization of some truth. Literary circles exist to smother the clarity of writing. Anarchist milieus to blunt the directness of direct action. Scientific milieus to withhold the implications of their research from the majority of people today. Sport milieus to contain in their gyms the various forms of life they should create. Particularly to be avoided are the cultural and activist circles. They are the old people's homes where all revolutionary desires traditionally go to die. The task of cultural circles is to spot nascent intensities and to explain away the sense of whatever it is you're doing, while the task of activist circles is to sap your energy for doing it. Activist milieus spread their diffuse web throughout the French territory, and are encountered on the path of every revolutionary development. They offer nothing but the story of their many defeats and the bitterness these have produced. Their exhaustion has made them incapable of seizing the possibilities of the present. Besides, to nurture their wretched passivity they talk far too much and this makes them unreliable when it comes to the police. Just as it's useless to expect anything from them, it's stupid to be disappointed by their sclerosis. It's best to just abandon this dead weight.

All milieus are counter-revolutionary because they are only concerned with the preservation of their sad comfort.

Form communes.

Communes come into being when people find each other, get on with each other, and decide on a common path. The commune is perhaps what gets decided at the very moment when we would normally part ways. It's the joy of an encounter that survives its expected end. It's what makes us say "we," and makes that an event. What's strange isn't that people who are attuned to each other form communes, but that they remain separated. Why shouldn't communes proliferate everywhere? In every factory, every street, every village, every school. At long last, the reign of the base committees!

Communes that accept being what they are, where they are. And if possible, a multiplicity of communes that will displace the institutions of society: family, school, union, sports club, etc. Communes that aren't afraid, beyond their specifically political activities, to organize themselves for the material and moral survival of each of their members and of all those around them who remain adrift. Communes that would not define themselves—as collectives tend to do—by what's inside and what's outside them, but by the density of the ties at their core. Not by their membership, but by the spirit that animates them.

A commune forms every time a few people, freed of their individual straitjackets, decide to rely only on themselves and measure their strength against reality. Every wildcat strike is a commune; every building occupied collectively and on a clear basis is a commune. The action committees of 1968 were communes, as were the slave maroons in the United States, or Radio Alice in Bologna in 1977. Every commune seeks to be its own base. It seeks to dissolve the question of needs. It seeks to break all economic dependency and all political subjugation; it degenerates into a milieu the moment it loses contact with the truths on which it is founded. There are all kinds of communes that wait neither for the numbers nor the means to get organized, and even less for the "right moment"—which never arrives.

GET ORGANIZED

Get organized in order to no longer have to work.

We know that individuals are possessed of so little life that they have to *earn a living*, to sell their time in exchange for a modicum of social existence. Personal time for social existence: such is work, such is the market. From the outset, the time of the commune eludes work, it doesn't function according to that scheme—it prefers others. Groups of Argentine *piqueteros* collectively extort a sort of local welfare conditioned by a few hours of work; they don't clock their hours, they put their benefits in common and acquire clothing workshops, a bakery, putting in place the gardens that they need.

The commune needs money, but not because we need to earn a living. All communes have their black markets. There are plenty of hustles. Aside from welfare, there are various benefits, disability money, accumulated student aid, subsidies drawn off fictitious childbirths, all kinds of trafficking, and so many other means that arise with every mutation of control. It's not for us to defend them, or to install ourselves in these temporary shelters or to preserve them as a privilege for those in the know. The important thing is to cultivate and spread this necessary disposition towards fraud, and to share its innovations. For communes, the question of work is only posed in relation to other already existing incomes. And we shouldn't forget all the useful knowledge that can be acquired through certain trades, professions and well-positioned jobs.

The exigency of the commune is to free up the most time for the most people. And we're not just talking about the *number of hours* free of any wage-labor exploitation. Liberated time doesn't mean a vacation. Vacant time, dead time, the time of emptiness and the fear of emptiness—this is the time of work. There will be no more time to *fill*, but a liberation of energy that no "time" contains; lines that take shape, that accentuate each other, that we can follow at our leisure, to their ends, until we see them cross with others.

Plunder, cultivate, fabricate.

Some former MetalEurop employees become bank robbers rather than prison guards. Some EDF employees show friends and family how to rig the electricity meters. Commodities that "fell off the back of a truck" are sold left and right. A world that so openly proclaims its cynicism can't expect much loyalty from proletarians.

On the one hand, a commune can't bank on the "welfare state" being around forever, and on the other, it can't count on living for long off shoplifting, nighttime dumpster diving at supermarkets or in the warehouses of the industrial zones, misdirecting government subsidies, ripping off insurance companies and other frauds, in a word: plunder. So it has to consider how to continually increase the level and scope of its self-organization. Nothing would be more logical than using the lathes, milling machines, and photocopiers sold at a discount after a factory closure to support a conspiracy against commodity society.

The feeling of imminent collapse is everywhere so strong these days that it would be hard to enumerate all of the current experiments in matters of construction, energy, materials, illegality or agriculture. There's a whole set of skills and techniques just waiting to be plundered and ripped from their humanistic, street-culture, or eco-friendly trappings. Yet this group of experiments is but one part of all of the intuitions, the know-how, and the ingenuity found in slums that will have to be deployed if we intend to repopulate the metropolitan desert and ensure the viability of an insurrection beyond its first stages.

How will we communicate and move about during a total interruption of the flows? How will we restore food production in rural areas to the point where they can once again support the population density that they had sixty years ago? How will we transform concrete spaces into urban vegetable gardens, as Cuba has done in order to withstand both the American embargo and the liquidation of the USSR?

Training and learning.

What are we left with, having used up most of the leisure authorized by market democracy? What was it that made us go jogging on a Sunday morning? What keeps all these karate fanatics, these DIY, fishing, or mycology freaks going? What, if not the need to fill up some totally idle time, to reconstitute their labor power or "health capital"? Most recreational activities could easily be stripped of their absurdity and become something else. Boxing has not always been limited to the staging of spectacular matches. At the beginning of the 20th century, as China was carved up by hordes of colonists and starved by long droughts, hundreds of thousands of its poor peasants organized themselves into countless open-air boxing clubs, in order to take back what the colonists and the rich had taken from them. This was the Boxer Rebellion. It's never too early to learn and practice what less pacified, less predictable times might require of us. Our dependence on the metropolis—on its medicine, its agriculture, its police—is so great at present that we can't attack it without putting ourselves in danger. An unspoken awareness of this vulnerability accounts for the spontaneous self-limitation of today's social movements, and explains our fear of crises and our desire for "security." It's for this reason that strikes have usually traded the prospect of revolution for a return to normalcy. Escaping this fate calls for a long and consistent process of apprenticeship, and for multiple, massive experiments. It's a question of knowing how to fight, to pick locks, to set broken bones and treat sicknesses; how to build a pirate radio transmitter; how to set up street kitchens; how to aim straight; how to gather together scattered knowledge and set up wartime agronomics; understand plankton biology; soil composition; study the way plants interact; get to know possible uses for and connections with our immediate environment as well as the limits we can't go beyond without exhausting it. We must start today, in preparation for the days when we'll need more than just a symbolic portion of our nourishment and care.

Create territories. Multiply zones of opacity.

More and more reformists today agree that with "the approach of peak oil," and in order to "reduce greenhouse gas emissions," we will need to "relocalize the economy," encourage regional supply lines, small distribution circuits, renounce easy access to imports from far away, etc. What they forget is that what characterizes everything that's done in a local economy is that it's done *under the table*, in an "informal" way; that this simple ecological measure of relocalizing the economy implies nothing less than total freedom from state control. Or else total submission to it.

Today's territory is the product of many centuries of police operations. People have been pushed out of their fields, then their streets, then their neighborhoods, and finally from the hallways of their buildings, in the demented hope of containing all life between the four sweating walls of privacy. The territorial question isn't the same for us as it is for the state. For us it's not about *possessing* territory. Rather, it's a matter of increasing the density of the communes, of circulation, and of solidarities to the point that the territory becomes unreadable, opaque to all authority. We don't want to occupy the territory, we want to *be* the territory.

Every practice brings a territory into existence—a dealing territory, or a hunting territory; a territory of child's play, of lovers, of a riot; a territory of farmers, ornithologists, or *flaneurs*. The rule is simple: the more territories there are superimposed on a given zone, the more circulation there is between them, the harder it will be for power to get a handle on them. Bistros, print shops, sports facilities, wastelands, second-hand book stalls, building rooftops, improvised street markets, kebab shops and garages can all easily be used for purposes other than their official ones if enough complicities come together in them. Local self-organization superimposes its own geography over the state cartography, scrambling and blurring it: it produces its own secession.

Travel. Open our own lines of communication.

The principle of communes is not to counter the metropolis and its mobility with local slowness and rootedness. The expansive movement of commune formation should surreptitiously overtake the movement of the metropolis. We don't have to reject the possibilities of travel and communication that the commercial infrastructure offers; we just have to know their limits. We just have to be prudent, innocuous. Visits in person are more secure, leave no trace, and forge much more consistent connections than any list of contacts on the internet. The privilege many of us enjoy of being able to "circulate freely" from one end of the continent to the other, and even across the world without too much trouble, is not a negligible asset when it comes to communication between pockets of conspiracy. One of the charms of the metropolis is that it allows Americans, Greeks, Mexicans, and Germans to meet furtively in Paris for the time it takes to discuss strategy.

Constant movement between friendly communes is one of the things that keeps them from drying up and from the inevitability of abandonment. Welcoming comrades, keeping abreast of their initiatives, reflecting on their experiences and making use of new techniques they've developed does more good for a commune than sterile self-examinations behind closed doors. It would be a mistake to underestimate how much can be decisively worked out over the course of evenings spent comparing views on the war in progress.

Remove all obstacles, one by one.

It's well known that the streets teem with incivilities. Between what they are and what they should be stands the centripetal force of the police, doing their best to restore order to them; and on the other side there's us, the opposite centrifugal movement. We can't help but delight in the fits of anger and disorder wherever they erupt. It's not surprising that these national festivals that aren't really celebrating anything anymore are now systematically going bad. Whether sparkling or dilapidated, the urban fixtures—but where do they begin? where do they end?—embody our common dispossession. Persevering in their nothingness, they ask for nothing more than to return to that state for good. Take a look at what surrounds us: all this will have its final hour. The metropolis suddenly takes on an air of nostalgia, like a field of ruins.

All the incivilities of the streets should become methodical and systematic, converging in a diffuse, effective guerrilla war that restores us to our ungovernability, our primordial unruliness. It's disconcerting to some that this same lack of discipline figures so prominently among the recognized military virtues of resistance fighters. In fact though, rage and politics should never have been separated. Without the first, the second is lost in discourse; without the second the first exhausts itself in howls. When words like *"enragés"* and *"exaltés"* resurface in politics they're always greeted with warning shots.[1]

As for methods, let's adopt the following principle from sabotage: a minimum of risk in taking the action, a minimum of time, and maximum damage. As for strategy, we will remember that an obstacle that has been cleared away, leaving a liberated but uninhabited space, is easily replaced by another obstacle, one that offers more resistance and is harder to attack.

No need to dwell too long on the three types of workers' sabotage: reducing the speed of work, from "easy does it" pacing to the "work-to-rule" strike; breaking the machines, or hindering their function; and divulging company secrets. Broadened to the dimensions of the whole social factory, the principles of sabotage can be applied to both production and circulation. The technical infrastructure of the metropolis is vulnerable. Its flows amount to more than the transportation of people and commodities.

---

1. The *enragés* and *exaltés* were both radical groups in the French revolution.

Information and energy circulate via wire networks, fibers and channels, and these can be attacked. Nowadays sabotaging the social machine with any real effect involves reappropriating and reinventing the ways of interrupting its networks. How can a TGV line or an electrical network be rendered useless? How does one find the weak points in computer networks, or scramble radio waves and fill screens with white noise?

As for serious obstacles, it's wrong to imagine them invulnerable to all destruction. The promethean element in all of this boils down to a certain use of fire, all blind voluntarism aside. In 356 BC, Erostratus burned down the temple of Artemis, one of the seven wonders of the world. In our time of utter decadence, the only thing imposing about temples is the dismal truth that *they are already ruins*.

Annihilating this nothingness is hardly a sad task. It gives action a fresh demeanor. Everything suddenly coalesces and makes sense—space, time, friendship. We must use all means at our disposal and rethink their uses—we ourselves being means. Perhaps, in the misery of the present, "fucking it all up" will serve—not without reason—as the last collective seduction.

Flee visibility. Turn anonymity into an offensive position.

In a demonstration, a union member tears the mask off of an anonymous person who has just broken a window. "Take responsibility for what you're doing instead of hiding yourself." But to be visible is to be exposed, that is to say above all, vulnerable. When leftists everywhere continually make their cause more "visible"—whether that of the homeless, of women, or of undocumented immigrants—in hopes that it will get dealt with, they're doing exactly the contrary of what must be done. Not making ourselves visible, but instead turning the anonymity to which we've been relegated to our advantage, and through conspiracy, nocturnal or faceless actions, creating an invulnerable position of attack. The fires of November 2005 offer a model for this. No leader, no demands, no organization, but words, gestures, complicities. To be socially nothing is not a humiliating condition, the source of some tragic lack of recognition—from whom do we seek recognition?—but is on the contrary the condition for maximum freedom of action. Not claiming your illegal actions, only attaching to them some fictional acronym—we still remember the ephemeral BAFT (*Brigade Anti-Flic des Tarterêts*)[2]—is a way to preserve that freedom. Quite obviously, one of the regime's first defensive maneuvers was the creation of a "*banlieue*" subject, to be treated as the author of

---

2. Tarterêts is a banlieue in the Essonne region of France. The "Tarterêts Anti-Cop Brigade" was a name that was employed to claim responsibility for actions against police in this area in the '80s.

the "riots of November 2005." Just looking at the faces on some of this society's *somebodies* illustrates why there's such joy in being nobody.

Visibility must be avoided. But a force that gathers in the shadows can't avoid it forever. Our appearance as a force must be reserved for the opportune moment. The longer we avoid visibility, the stronger we'll be when it catches up with us. And once we become visible our days will be numbered. Either we will be in a position to break its hold in short order, or we'll be crushed in no time.

Organize self-defense.

We live under an occupation, under *police* occupation. Undocumented immigrants are rounded up in the middle of the street, unmarked police cars patrol the boulevards, metropolitan districts are pacified with techniques forged in the colonies, the Minister of the Interior makes declarations of war on "gangs" that remind us of the Algerian war—we are reminded of it every day. These are reasons enough to no longer let ourselves be beaten down, reasons enough to organize our self-defense.

To the extent that it grows and radiates, a commune begins to see the operations of power target that which constitutes it. These counterattacks take the form of seduction, of recuperation, and as a last resort, brute force. For a commune, self-defense must be a collective fact, as much practical as theoretical. Preventing an arrest, gathering quickly and in large numbers against eviction attempts and sheltering one of our own, will not be superfluous reflexes in coming times. We cannot ceaselessly reconstruct our bases from scratch. Let's stop denouncing repression and instead prepare to confront it.

It's not a simple affair, for we expect a surge in police work being done by the population itself—everything from snitching to occasional participation in citizens' militias. The police forces blend in with the crowd. The ubiquitous model of police intervention, even in riot situations, is now the cop in civilian clothes. The effectiveness of the police during the last anti-CPE demonstrations was a result of plainclothes officers mixing among us and waiting for an incident before revealing who they are: gas, nightsticks, tazers, detainment; all in strict coordination with demonstration stewards. The mere possibility of their presence was enough to create suspicion amongst the demonstrators—who's who?—and to paralyze action. If we agree that a demonstration is not merely a way to stand and be counted but a means of action, we have to equip ourselves with better resources to unmask plainclothes officers, chase them off, and if need be snatch back those they're trying to arrest.

The police are not invincible in the streets, they simply have the means to organize, train, and continually test new weapons. Our weapons, on the other hand, are always rudimentary, cobbled-together, and often improvised on the spot. Ours certainly can't hope to match theirs in firepower, but can be used to hold them at a distance, redirect attention, exercise psychological pressure or force passage and gain ground by surprise. None of the innovations in urban anti-guerilla warfare that are being taught in the French police academies are adequate to respond rapidly to a moving multiplicity that can strike a number of places at once and that tries to always keep the initiative.

Communes are obviously vulnerable to surveillance and police investigations, to policing technologies and intelligence gathering. The waves of arrests of anarchists in Italy and of eco-warriors in the US were made possible by wiretapping. Everyone detained by the police now has his or her DNA sampled and added to an ever more complete profile. A squatter from Barcelona was caught because he left fingerprints on fliers he was distributing. Tracking methods are becoming better and better, mostly through biometric techniques. And if the distribution of electronic identity cards is instituted, our task will just be that much more difficult. The Paris Commune found a partial solution to the keeping of records: they burned down City Hall, destroying all the public records and vital statistics. We still need to find the means to permanently destroy computerized databases.

INSURRECTION

The commune is the basic unit of partisan reality. An insurrectional surge may be nothing more than a multiplication of communes, their coming into contact and forming of ties. As events unfold, communes will either merge into larger entities or fragment. The difference between a band of brothers and sisters bound "for life" and the gathering of many groups, committees and gangs for organizing the supply and self-defense of a neighborhood or even a region in revolt, is only a difference of scale, they are all communes.

A commune tends by its nature towards self-sufficiency and considers money, internally, as something foolish and ultimately out of place. The power of money is to connect those who are unconnected, to link strangers *as strangers* and thus, by making everything equivalent, to put everything into circulation.

The cost of money's capacity to connect everything is the superficiality of the connection, where deception is the rule. Distrust is the basis of the credit relation. The reign of money is, therefore, always the reign of control. The practical abolition of money will happen only with the extension of communes. Communes must be extended while making sure they do not exceed a certain size, beyond which they lose touch with themselves and give rise, almost without fail, to a dominant caste. It would be preferable for the commune to split up and to spread in that way, avoiding such an unfortunate outcome.

The uprising of Algerian youth that erupted across all of Kabylia in the spring of 2001 managed to take over almost the entire territory, attacking police stations, courthouses and every representation of the state, generalizing the revolt to the point of compelling the unilateral retreat of the forces of order and physically preventing the elections. The movement's strength was in the diffuse complementarity of its components—only partially represented by the interminable and hopelessly male-dominated village assemblies and other popular committees. The "communes" of this still-simmering insurrection had many faces: the young hotheads in helmets lobbing gas canisters at the riot police from the rooftop of a building in Tizi Ouzou; the wry smile of an old resistance fighter draped in his burnous; the spirit of the women in the mountain villages, stubbornly carrying on with the traditional farming, without which the blockades of the region's economy would never have been as constant and systematic as they were.

Make the most of every crisis.

"So it must be said, too, that we won't be able to treat the entire French population. Choices will have to be made." This is how a virology expert sums up, in a September 7, 2005 article in *Le Monde*, what would happen in the event of a bird flu pandemic. "Terrorist threats," "natural disasters," "virus warnings," "social movements" and "urban violence" are, for society's managers, so many moments of instability where they reinforce their power, by the selection of those who please them and the elimination of those who make things difficult. Clearly these are, in turn, opportunities for other forces to consolidate or strengthen one another as they take the other side.

The interruption of the flow of commodities, the suspension of normality (it's sufficient to see how social life returns in a building suddenly deprived of electricity to imagine what life could become in a city deprived of everything) and police control liberate potentialities for self-organization unthinkable in other circumstances. People are not blind to this. The revolutionary workers' movement understood it well, and took advantage of the crises of the bourgeois economy to gather strength. Today, Islamic parties are strongest when they've been able to intelligently compensate for the weakness of the state—as when they provided aid after the earthquake in Boumerdes, Algeria, or in the daily assistance offered the population of southern Lebanon after it was ravaged by the Israeli army.

As we mentioned above, the devastation of New Orleans by hurricane Katrina gave a certain fringe of the North American anarchist movement the opportunity to achieve an unfamiliar cohesion by rallying all those who refused to be forcefully evacuated. Street kitchens require building up provisions beforehand; emergency medical aid requires the acquisition of necessary knowledge and materials, as does the setting up of pirate radios. The political richness of such experiences is assured by the joy they contain, the way they transcend individual stoicism, and their manifestation of a tangible reality that escapes the daily ambience of order and work.

In a country like France, where radioactive clouds stop at the border and where we aren't afraid to build a cancer research center on the former site of a nitrogen fertilizer factory that has been condemned by the EU's industrial safety agency, we should count less on "natural" crises than on social ones. It is usually up to the social movements to interrupt the normal course of the disaster. Of course, in recent years the various strikes were primarily opportunities for the government and corporate management to test their ability to maintain a larger and larger "minimum service," to the point of reducing the work stoppage to a purely symbolic dimension, causing little more damage than a snowstorm or a suicide on the railroad tracks. By going against established activist practices through the systematic occupation of institutions and obstinate blockading, the high-school students' struggle of 2005 and the struggle against the CPE-law reminded us of the ability of large movements to cause trouble and carry out diffuse offensives. In all the affinity groups they spawned and left in their wake, we glimpsed the conditions that allow social movements to become a locus for the emergence of new communes.

Sabotage every representative authority.
Spread the talk.
Abolish general assemblies.

The first obstacle every social movement faces, long before the police proper, are the unions and the entire micro-bureaucracy whose job it is to control the struggle. Communes, collectives and gangs are naturally distrustful of these structures. That's why the parabureaucrats have for the past twenty years been inventing coordination committees and spokes councils that seem more innocent because they lack an established label, but are in fact the ideal terrain for their maneuvers. When a stray collective makes an attempt at autonomy, they won't be satisfied until they've drained the attempt of all content by preventing any real question from being addressed. They get fierce and worked up not out of passion for debate but out of a passion for shutting it down. And when their dogged defense of apathy finally does the collective in, they explain its failure by citing a lack of political consciousness. It must be noted that in France the militant youth are well versed in the art of political manipulation, thanks largely to the frenzied activity of various Trotskyist factions. They could not be expected to learn the lesson of the conflagration of November 2005: that coordinations are unnecessary where coordination *exists*, organizations aren't needed when people organize themselves.

Another reflex is to call a general assembly at the slightest sign of movement, and vote. This is a mistake. The business of voting and deciding a winner is enough to turn the assembly into a nightmare, into a theater where all the various little pretenders to power confront each other. Here we suffer from the bad example of bourgeois parliaments. An assembly is not a place for decisions but for *talk*, for free speech exercised without a goal.

The need to assemble is as constant among humans as the necessity of making decisions is rare. Assembling corresponds to the joy of feeling a common power. Decisions are vital only in emergency situations, where the exercise of democracy is already compromised. The rest of the time, "the democratic character of decision making" is only a problem for the fanatics of process. It's not a matter of critiquing assemblies or abandoning them, but of liberating the speech, gestures, and interplay of beings that take place within them. We just have to see that each person comes to an assembly not only with a point of view or a motion, but with desires, attachments, capacities, forces, sadnesses and a certain disposition toward others, an openness. If we manage to set aside the fantasy of a General Assembly and replace it with an *assembly of presences*, if we manage to foil the constantly renewed temptation of hegemony, if we stop making the decision our final aim, then there is a chance for a kind of *critical mass*, one of those moments of collective crystallization where a decision suddenly takes hold of beings, completely or only in part.

The same goes for deciding on actions. By starting from the principle that "the action in question should govern the assembly's agenda" we make both vigorous debate and effective action impossible. A large assembly made up of people who don't know each other is obliged to call on action specialists, that is, to abandon action for the sake of its control. On the one hand, people with mandates are by definition hindered in their actions, on the other hand, nothing hinders them from deceiving everyone.

There's no ideal form of action. What's essential is that action assume a certain form, that it give rise to a form instead of having one imposed on it. This presupposes a shared political and geographical position—like the sections of the Paris Commune during the French Revolution—as well as the circulation of a shared knowledge. As for deciding on actions, the principle could be as follows: each person should do their own reconnaissance, the information would then be put together, and the decision will occur to us rather than being made by us. The circulation of knowledge cancels hierarchy; it equalizes by raising up. Proliferating horizontal communication is also the best form of coordination among different communes, the best way to put an end to hegemony.

Block the economy, but measure our blocking power by our level of self-organization.

At the end of June 2006 in the State of Oaxaca, the occupations of city halls multiply, and insurgents occupy public buildings. In certain communes, mayors are kicked out, official vehicles are requisitioned. A month later, access is cut off to certain hotels and tourist compounds. Mexico's Minister of Tourism speaks of a disaster "comparable to hurricane Wilma." A few years earlier, blockades had become the main form of action of the revolt in Argentina, with different local groups helping each other by blocking this or that major road, and continually threatening, through their joint action, to paralyze the entire country if their demands were not met. For years such threats have been a powerful lever for railway workers, truck drivers, and electrical and gas supply workers. The movement against the CPE in France did not hesitate to block train stations, ring roads, factories, highways, supermarkets and even airports. In Rennes, only three hundred people were needed to shut down the main access road to the town for hours and cause a 40-kilometer long traffic jam.

Jam everything—this will be the first reflex of all those who rebel against the present order. In a delocalized economy where companies function according to "just-in-time" production, where value derives from connectedness to the network, where the highways are links in the chain of dematerialized production which moves from subcontractor to subcontractor and from there to another factory for assembly, to block circulation is to block production as well.

But a blockade is only as effective as the insurgents' capacity to supply themselves and to communicate, as effective as the self-organization of the different communes. How will we feed ourselves once everything is paralyzed? Looting stores, as in Argentina, has its limits; as large as the temples of consumption are, they are not bottomless pantries. Acquiring the skills to provide, over time, for one's own basic subsistence implies appropriating the necessary means of its production. And in this regard, it seems pointless to wait any longer. Letting two percent of the population produce the food of all the others—the situation today—is both a historical and a strategic anomaly.

Liberate territory from police occupation.
Avoid direct confrontation, if possible.

"This business shows that we are not dealing with young people making social demands, but with individuals who are declaring war on the Republic," noted a lucid cop about recent clashes. The push to liberate territory from police occupation is already underway, and can count on the endless reserves of resentment that the forces of order have marshaled against it. Even the "social movements" are gradually being seduced by the riots, just like the festive crowds in Rennes who fought the cops every Thursday night in 2005, or those in Barcelona who destroyed a shopping district during a *botellón*. The movement against the CPE witnessed the recurrent return of the Molotov cocktail. But on this front certain *banlieues* remain unsurpassed. Specifically, when it comes to the technique they've been perfecting for some time now: the surprise attack. Like the one on October 13, 2006 in Epinay. A private-security team headed out after getting a report of something stolen from a car. When they arrived, one of the security guards "found himself blocked by two vehicles parked diagonally across the street and by more than thirty people carrying metal bars and pistols who threw stones at the

vehicle and used tear gas against the police officers."
On a smaller scale, think of all the local police stations attacked in the night: broken windows, burnt-out cop cars.

One of the results of these recent movements is the understanding that henceforth a real demonstration has to be "wild," not declared in advance to the police. Having the *choice of terrain*, we can, like the Black Bloc of Genoa in 2001, bypass the red zones and avoid direct confrontation. By choosing our own trajectory, we can lead the cops, including unionist and pacifist ones, rather than being herded by them. In Genoa we saw a thousand determined people push back entire buses full of *carabinieri*, then set their vehicles on fire. The important thing is not to be better armed but to take the initiative. Courage is nothing, confidence in your own courage is everything. Having the initiative helps.

Everything points, nonetheless, toward a conception of direct confrontations as that which pins down opposing forces, buying us time and allowing us to attack elsewhere—even nearby. The fact that we cannot prevent a confrontation from occurring doesn't prevent us from making it into a simple diversion. Even more than to actions, we must commit ourselves to their coordination. Harassing the police means that by forcing them to be everywhere they can no longer be effective anywhere.

Every act of harassment revives this truth, spoken in 1842: "The life of the police agent is painful; his position in society is as humiliating and despised as crime itself… Shame and infamy encircle him from all sides, society expels him, isolates him as a pariah, society spits out its disdain for the police agent along with his pay, without remorse, without regrets, without pity… The police badge that he carries in his pocket documents his shame." On November 21, 2006, firemen demonstrating in Paris attacked the riot police with hammers and injured fifteen of them. This by way of a reminder that wanting to "protect and serve" can never be an excuse for joining the police.

Take up arms. Do everything possible to make their use unnecessary. Against the army, the only victory is political.

There is no such thing as a peaceful insurrection. Weapons are necessary; it's a question of doing everything possible to make using them unnecessary. An insurrection is more about taking up arms and maintaining an "armed presence" than it is about armed struggle. We need to distinguish clearly between being armed and the use of arms. Weapons are a constant in revolutionary situations, but their use is infrequent and rarely decisive at key turning points: August 10th 1792, March 18th 1871, October 1917. When power is in the gutter, it's enough to walk over it.

Because of the distance that separates us from them, weapons have taken on a kind of double character of fascination and disgust that can be overcome only by handling them. An authentic pacifism cannot mean refusing weapons, but only refusing to use them. Pacifism without being able to fire a shot is nothing but the theoretical formulation of impotence. Such *a priori* pacifism is a kind of preventive disarmament, a pure police operation. In reality, the question of pacifism is serious only for those who have the ability to open fire. In this case, pacifism becomes a sign of power, since it's only in an extreme position of strength that we are freed from the need to fire.

From a strategic point of view, indirect, asymmetrical action seems the most effective kind, the one best suited to our time: you don't attack an occupying army frontally. That said, the prospect of Iraq-style urban guerilla warfare, dragging on with no possibility of taking the offensive, is more to be feared than to be desired. The *militarization* of civil war is the defeat of insurrection. The Reds had their victory in 1921, but the Russian Revolution was already lost.

We must consider two kinds of state reaction. One openly hostile, one more sly and democratic. The first calls for our out-and-out destruction, the second, a subtle but implacable hostility, seeks only to recruit us. We can be defeated both by dictatorship and by being reduced to opposing *only* dictatorship. Defeat consists as much in losing the war as in losing the *choice* of which war to wage. Both are possible, as was proven by Spain in 1936: the revolutionaries there were defeated twice-over, by fascism and by the Republic.

When things get serious, the army occupies the terrain. Whether or not it engages in combat is less certain. That would require that the state be committed to a bloodbath, which for now is no more than a threat, a bit like the threat of using nuclear weapons for the last fifty years. Though it has been wounded for a long while, the beast of the state is still dangerous. A massive crowd would be needed to challenge the army, invading its ranks and fraternizing with the soldiers. We need a March 18th, 1871. When the army is in the street, we have an insurrectionary situation. Once the army engages, the outcome is precipitated. Everyone finds themselves forced to take sides, to choose between anarchy and the fear of anarchy. An insurrection triumphs as a political force. It is not impossible to defeat an army politically.

Depose authorities at a local level.

The goal of any insurrection is to become irreversible. It becomes irreversible when you've defeated both authority and the need for authority, property and the taste for appropriation, hegemony and the desire for hegemony. That is why the insurrectionary process carries within itself the form of its victory, or that of its defeat. Destruction has never been enough to make things irreversible. What matters is how it's done. There are ways of destroying that unfailingly provoke the return of what has been crushed. Whoever wastes their energy on the corpse of an order can be sure that this will arouse the desire for vengeance. Thus, wherever the economy is blocked and the police are neutralized, it is important to invest as little pathos as possible in overthrowing the authorities. They must be deposed with the most scrupulous indifference and derision.

In times like these, the end of centralized revolutions reflects the decentralization of power. Winter Palaces still exist but they have been relegated to assaults by tourists rather than revolutionary hordes. Today it is possible to take over Paris, Rome, or Buenos Aires without it being a decisive victory. Taking over Rungis would certainly be more effective than taking over the Elysée Palace. Power is no longer concentrated in one point in the world; it is the world itself, its flows and its avenues, its people and its norms, its codes and its technologies. Power is the organization of the metropolis itself. It is the impeccable totality of the world of the commodity at each of its points. Anyone who defeats it locally sends a planetary shock wave through its networks. The riots that began in Clichy-sous-Bois filled more than one American household with joy, while the insurgents of Oaxaca found accomplices right in the heart of Paris. For France, the loss of centralized power signifies the end of Paris as the center of revolutionary activity. Every new movement since the strikes of 1995 has confirmed this. It's no longer in Paris that the most daring and consistent actions are carried out. To put it bluntly, Paris now stands out only as a target for raids, as a pure terrain to be plundered and ravaged. Brief and brutal incursions from the outside strike at the metropolitan flows at their point of maximum density. Rage streaks across this desert of fake abundance, then vanishes. A day will come when this capital and its horrible concretion of power will lie in majestic ruins, but it will be at the end of a process that will be far more advanced everywhere else.

All power to the communes!

In the subway, there's no longer any trace of the screen of embarrassment that normally impedes the gestures of the passengers. Strangers make conversation without making passes. A band of comrades conferring on a street corner. Much larger assemblies on the boulevards, absorbed in discussions. Surprise attacks mounted in city after city, day after day. A new military barracks has been sacked and burned to the ground. The evicted residents of a building have stopped negotiating with the mayor's office; they settle in. A company manager is inspired to blow away a handful of his colleagues in the middle of a meeting. There's been a leak of files containing the personal addresses of all the cops, together with those of prison officials, causing an unprecedented wave of sudden relocations. We carry our surplus goods into the old village bar and grocery store, and take what we lack. Some of us stay long enough to discuss the general situation and figure out the hardware we need for the machine shop. The radio keeps the insurgents informed of the retreat of the government forces. A rocket has just breached a wall of the Clairvaux prison. Impossible to say if it has been months or years since the "events" began. And the prime minister seems very alone in his appeals for calm.